Where T

Where There is Vision

The family story of
the Torch Trust for the Blind

Stella Heath

Marshall Pickering
in conjunction with
the Torch Trust for the Blind

*All proceeds from the sale of this book
will go to the work of The Torch Trust
for the Blind*

Marshall Morgan and Scott
Marshall Pickering
3 Beggarwood Lane, Basingstoke,
Hants RG23 7LP, UK

Illustrations by Paul A. F. Ferraby

ISBN: 0 551 01361 3

Printed in Great Britain by Anchor Brendon Ltd,
Tiptree, Colchester, Essex.

Contents

Preface

This book almost became an Unfinished Symphony. Since we started to put pen to paper in 1975, so many "waves and billows" have rolled over us as a family that we were left feeling bruised and breathless. Writing became too painful. The book project, which we knew should be tackled, was left in abeyance.

On several occasions friends had prodded us. "When are we going to have that next book?" We would smile and say, "When we have time". Yet, deep inside, we dreaded finding time to sift through what had been written already with the aid of a loving companion no longer with us. We felt too that words were so inadequate to convey our thoughts and feelings, and the new tender realisation of the Lord Jesus Christ which we had discovered.

Then I broke my ankle. I was only taking a quiet leisurely walk on the Langdales, when I slipped, and broke three bones. How can I describe those moments, sitting in the sun, on the grassy path, nursing a broken ankle, while a worried husband ran to get help? All I know is that I met with the Lord in all His love and tenderness. "It is I, be not afraid". And something that had been a deep-down hurt in my soul was suddenly gone. "Now, I want you to write that book", I felt the Lord was saying. And I found that I could.

During the next few weeks I *had* to sit down and organise my time around the writing. I had great help and encouragement from all the family at this time. In fact, I was almost spoiled by their love and concern. The hard slog of correcting, typing, re-writing and adjusting was shared by so many of my colleagues in the work.

I have been filled with praise as I have traced the Hand of God working in our family, and since my accident it has been a joy to write. I pray that, as a result, this book will be a joy to read.

S. G. Heath

Introduction

There is something fascinating about rivers, from the first tiny trickle of water bubbling up from the spring, to the wide, steady flow at the estuary. Rivers seem so alive, and, provided they are not polluted by man, they give life everywhere they flow. They bring nourishment to the sheep on the hillside, they irrigate the plains, they cool the air and refresh the traveller. Fishermen line their banks knowing that their waters abound with fish. And, under the surface, there is a whole world of aquatic life, balanced and beautiful, teeming with activity.

Rivers of life! Isn't that what the Lord Jesus Christ promised us that we should have flowing from us? (John 7:38).

The work which God is doing in the Torch Family is rather like a river. We saw the spring, and the tiny streamlet with which it began, in the book "The Opened Way". Then, as it flowed on, we looked into the higher reaches of the river in "The Torch Family". But like all living things, especially when the life-force is that of the Holy Spirit of God, the river has become wider, deeper and more far-reaching over these past years. This is why we have felt the need to write a sequel, "Where there is Vision", for God has led us into deeper ways with Himself, which we feel compelled to put into writing.

In this new book we have not repeated the story which is told in "The Torch Family", except that in the first chapter we quickly trace the river back to its source. The technicalities of Braille and Moon-type, the formulation of policies concerning administration and finance, are not dealt with in "Where there is Vision". We have, instead, tried to take an honest look at the river as it flows on. We have glimpses of the depths of God's love, and His life-giving power, as He ministers to human suffering. We see something of the blessings, the growth, the sparkles of joyfulness, and the deep, dark depths of suffering too. Yet the Living Water flows on abundantly, a full supply which is ours in Christ Jesus our Lord.

The river which flowed from the Sanctuary in Ezekiel's vision brought life and healing to dead places. The river which flows from Christ through His Church is destined to do the same. It is adequate for every need. Our prayer is that we may always be kept in the centre of its flow, and never drift into a backwater.

> "Like a river, glorious,
>   Is God's perfect peace;
>   Over all victorious
>   In its bright increase.
>   Perfect, yet it floweth
>   Fuller every day;
>   Perfect, yet it groweth
>   Deeper all the way."

CHAPTER 1 — THE STORY OF FIVE HOUSES

"Winscales". The signpost pointed up the hill towards a farm with a few cottages clustered round it. The sky was grey, and a keen wind was blowing in from the sea as we climbed up to House Number One.

To the left we could see the town of Workington; to the right, the grey mountain ranges of the Lake District. But it was not the view which claimed our attention so much as the weathered old house which crowned the hill, for it was here in Winscales House that Misses Eva and Ada Trench lived during the 1920's. As we stood at the front door and looked at the circular driveway, we could imagine the ladies standing there, in Sunday dress, waiting for the coachman to drive up.

Then, with unfailing regularity, they would enter the carriage, holding their beloved Bibles, and drive off to the meeting room in Workington, to enjoy a simple time of worship with the brethren there.

The sisters were deeply interested in the well-being of their servants, so it must have been a sorrow to them when they discovered that their coachman was losing his sight. We have no doubt they supported him in every way possible, helping him to adjust to the new limitations which blindness brought. This event particularly impressed Miss Eva with the great need there was among blind people. She decided to do something about it, and in 1931 she started to edit a tiny braille letter hardly big enough to be called a magazine, in an effort to share with blind people the most wonderful experience of all, the joy of accepting the Gospel of the Lord Jesus Christ.

We walked down the garden path and along the tree-lined "Ladies' Walk". How often, we wondered, did the sisters stroll here, talking and planning what to include in their next issue? It might have been here, under the trees, that they thought of the name "Torch".

Miss Ada's room overlooked the garden. Can we imagine her sorrow when her sister Eva died? Did she look out of this window and pray for strength to take up her sister's editorial work? She certainly received that strength, for she shouldered the burden faithfully until she was eighty-three years old.

By this time she had left Winscales and had moved to Brow Top in Workington itself. The old family house was sold, and became a Mines Rescue Station. But Miss Ada kept on faithfully, bent on rescue of another kind, from the pit of sin, and a darkness which was both physical and spiritual. There must have been times when the work was encouraging, but it was such a slender life-line with which to try to meet the needs of the blind of the world!

About this time Miss Trench formed the Blind Fund Trust, and with the aid of a far-seeing solicitor, drew up a Trust Deed which gave a glimpse into what she would have liked to have done. This was so comprehensive that it made a full allowance for any Christ-centred future development.

But Miss Ada was getting old and her health was far from good. She must often have prayed about the future of the work which had become so dear to her heart.

* * * * * *

Now we come to a very different scene from the quiet, orderly life of the Trench family. House Number Two was a semi-detached Victorian villa in Reigate, Surrey, and was the home of Ron and Stella Heath and their boisterous family of two boys and two girls. It would be hard to find any connection with Miss Ada and her work with the Blind Fund Trust.

The Reigate house was roomy and had a lovely view of Reigate Hill from the back windows. But the folk who formed the link with Winscales and Brow Top would not be particularly interested in the view. On any Sunday you could see groups of blind young people making their way to the old house in Reigate. Some who had a little sight would guide the totally blind up the path to the front door. The more venturesome of the blind boys would tap their way up to the door, using their white canes. Some of them were quite tastefully dressed; others seemed indifferent to their

3

appearance. They made themselves at home sitting on chairs, on the arms of chairs, on stools, or on the carpet. Some of them played the piano; others chatted freely to each other. They liked the old record player too, and were especially fond of one record: "It is No Secret what God can Do." Some of them even shed tears when this record was played.

This had all started because one blind girl had come down to the Heaths' home to a Club, and had become a true believer in the Lord Jesus Christ. The change in her life was immediately noticed by the Principal and staff at "Hethersett", the Royal National Institute for the Blind Vocational Assessment Centre on the other side of the Common. They asked the Heath family to help them with other young people, to integrate them with their own Youth Group and Church, and to give them a taste of home life. So the Heath family held "Open House" every Sunday afternoon and evening. It was never a meeting, or a preaching session, but the young folk were encouraged to talk freely and honestly together. Soon a number of them came to know Jesus Christ as Saviour. This is why they loved that record,

> "It is no secret what God can do;
> What He's done for others, He'll do for you".

Tea time was fun; sandwiches were eaten with teenage eagerness, and an amazing amount of tea was drunk. All the time, God was doing a quiet yet real work in their hearts. Ron and Stella Heath tried to find some literature in braille which would help these young people to understand more about the Christian life. They found to their amazement that there was almost nothing suitable to be obtained anywhere. Then they heard of "Torch", Miss Trench's magazine.

Meanwhile, Miss Ada Trench had become very ill. She was interested in the happenings at Reigate and asked the Heath family to write and tell her all about them. Mrs. Heath did so, including a little about their own children, Rosemary, Andrew, Philip and Marjorie too. Soon afterwards Miss Trench asked them to take over the editorship of "Torch". Miss Trench told her readers about this change, in the "Torch" magazine for May 1959. Before most of the readers

4

received their copy, Miss Trench had gone to be with the Lord.

So that is how we, Ron and Stella Heath, were brought into touch with the blind family which later became known as "The Torch Family".

House Number Two was large, as semi-detached family houses go. It had seven bedrooms, a large lounge, dining-room and morning room, a butler's pantry and a scullery. To begin with, we put up shelves in the butler's pantry to hold the few books which were sent down from Miss Trench's home. Then we started to collect others to make a braille and moon library. We heard of one or two folk who were willing to transcribe the books from print to braille, so that other Christian titles could be added to the library. They were not proof-read in those days, but were bound and put straight on to the shelves. At first these books were borrowed by people who came to the house, but gradually the library began to develop into a postal service. Those precious individually-brailled volumes were carefully wrapped in corrugated cardboard and brown paper in those early days! Meanwhile, the "Torch" magazine was being increased in size, and the circulation was beginning to rise. For years it had been brailled by friends in Sutton, who embossed the zinc plates on an old, electrified hand-frame. The impressions were transferred to paper by passing through the rollers of a wringer!

Soon the butler's pantry was overcrowded, so we pulled down a disused chimney to make room for a larger area of shelving in the morning-room. This soon began to fill up with bulky volumes of braille and moon books, and a few little tracts which we had laboriously brailled ourselves.

Still the work grew, until the lounge had to be taken over and turned into a library and office. The dining-room then became the family lounge, and the morning-room became the dining-room. "Torch" had begun to grow!

All this time Ron was travelling up to London each day, leaving home at 7.30 a.m. and returning at 6.30 in the evening. He used the travelling time profitably, for it was as he was sitting in the train on his daily journey to town, that he began to learn braille. Then his Department was de-centralised by the Bank, and he was asked to move to Crawley. The family decided that this was the time for them to move—which brings us to House Number Three.

* * * * * *

Crawley New Town—what a change from the mature trees and the beautiful scenery of Reigate! It wasn't easy for the family to get used to it, and it meant leaving the work among the blind young folk in other hands. But it gave more time to spend on braille and other demands made by the growing literature work of "Torch". As Crawley was not too far away from Reigate, some of the blind young people were still able to come to us for weekends, so that the personal side of the work never completely stopped.

From the first, there were difficulties. It is one thing to move from a large old seven-bedroomed house to a modern four-bedroomed one, but when you have a braille library, brailling machines, typewriters, an ever-growing filing system, and the pressing thought that much more ought to be done, then headaches are multiplied. We decided to buy a 12 ft. x 20 ft. hut to put at the end of the garden, well away from neighbours, so that the library and the office could be kept separate from the house. In fact, we stipulated firmly that the "Torch" work must stay in the hut and not invade the house. In those days we did not think of it as the total commitment which God had intended it to be.

Then came the first problem. Crawley Council did not want us to have a hut in the garden! So at first we put the precious braille volumes in the disused gallery of the old building of Three Bridges Free Church. Twice a week we would go up to the dark, dusty gallery to change the books returned by readers. With the aid of a torch we would search for new titles to send them. Then we loaded them, in their canvas bags, on to a pram complete with baby, and trundled them round to the nearest Post Office.

Eventually, after many letters and much hard work by Mr. Gladstone Moore, then Honorary Minister of Three Bridges Free Church, we were given permission to erect the hut. At

6

last, in December 1962, we had a service of dedication and thanksgiving for the very first property owned by Torch. One of the speakers on that occasion took as his text, "Where there is no vision, the people perish". Of course, he meant spiritual vision. This special time of thanksgiving developed into our yearly Thanksgiving Service. Each year, as the time has come round for Thanksgiving, we have been aware of new and wider visions, and so much for which to praise and thank the Lord!

The work grew rapidly at Crawley. We were brought in touch with more and more people who were starved of the Bread of Life because they could not read. It was also at this time that the Lord began to draw together volunteers to help us with the work. Mr. Moore became our Chairman; it was at Crawley that Joy Alexander, our Treasurer, joined us; Joan and Ken Blackmore too gave much of their free time to help. Peter and Rosemary Wootten began their long association with us. It was a time of growth, not only of the work, but also of the fellowship as we prayed and worked together. We began to have opportunities to visit Clubs and Homes for blind folk, and particularly the deaf-blind. Although we had very little spare room in the house, we did manage to have a few deaf-blind folk to stay for holidays. Some of these had terribly big problems, and we began to see the need for a personal ministry amongst them.

It was not long before the literature side of "Torch" invaded the house. A brailling machine and a wringer were bought, and we began to produce our own braille. Consequently, our desks had to come up to the house. This was but the beginning! Large print began to be produced, and a certain amount of tape work was started. In the end we had to turn the garage into an office, build a recording room, and use every available space in loft and bedroom for storage. After six years, House Number Three was obviously not big enough!

We were now faced with the necessity for full commitment to the work, for the only way we could get a bigger house was to hand over the one we owned to provide some of the capital. Were we willing to trust the Lord for our security, even if it meant owning nothing, but giving it all to Him? It was not an easy decision, yet it was the only obvious one. After all, how could we sing and preach that Christ was all that we needed if we were clinging on to our house for the sake of security? And how could we hope to encourage others in a walk of faith, if we ourselves were not prepared for it?

So, with many prayers for guidance and strength, we were introduced to House Number Four—the very first Torch House—in the village of Hurstpierpoint, Sussex.

* * * * * *

The House at Hurstpierpoint had formerly been used by the Church Army as a Rest Home for their Sisters, and the lovely little chapel was one of the blessings which we inherited from them. We entered an atmosphere of prayer and love when we came to Torch House, just the right setting for the new aspects of the work which were to be revealed to us.

There was plenty of room at the Hurstpierpoint house; a beautiful chapel, a large 20 ft. x 30 ft. lounge, and fifteen small bedrooms, a reasonable kitchen, and a very big hut in the garden which would do for office and literature work, made us convinced that we had all the room we should ever need. True, the hut tilted a little, so that when we sat at our desks the pencils tended to roll off. True, that hut leaked unpredictably in wet, windy weather; we became skilled at using umbrellas in certain places, and bowls to collect the drips. That hut could be cold in winter, and we were so glad of the knitted blankets which were given to us. We wore them as skirts, shawls and saris—any way that would give us enough warmth to carry on in cold weather!

The work grew tremendously. Young blind people in need started to come to stay for long or short periods. Many of them found peace by trusting the Lord Jesus; some stayed on and eventually joined the staff, thus passing on to others the help which they had received. The only thing which didn't grow was the house! Six years after we had moved into Torch House, Hurstpierpoint, we faced the need for another move! Our staff numbered thirty-five by this time; we had a mobile home parked in the drive for the boys to sleep in, single bedrooms were now used as doubles, and a number of staff were living in the villages around. The large hut, and the small hut which we had brought from Crawley, were filled to capacity. Large print was being produced in a downstairs bedroom, and the braille press was operating in the sun lounge. But the worst-hit was the recording section. The cassette work was taking up all the room in the little recording booth, so the talking book copying (the latest development) had to be done on two trolleys in the dining-room, which were wheeled away at meal-times. At houseparty times too, the house was very inadequate.

We asked searching questions. One was, "Why did God move us here, if He knew we would outgrow it in six years?" I believe that the Lord wanted us to be a *family,* not an institution, so He directed us to this house first, in which to form our routine and our pattern for family worship. This meant. that these had the touch of home, which was so necessary when dealing with young people whose biggest earthly lack was that of a loving home-life. Yes, in many ways, we are so glad that we started to live as the "Torch Family" in a house the size of the one at Hurstpierpoint.

A move was inevitable, and so we began our search for House Number Five—a larger home for our growing family.

CHAPTER 2 — HALLATON HALL

It was at a Bible study in a friendly Anglican church where we met the contact who put us in touch with Hallaton Hall. She came to us, face alight with fellowship, in the dress of a nun. We discovered that she was actually Mother Superior of a local Roman Catholic convent. "Some of our convents are closing down", she said. "There may well be one which is suitable for you. I will send you details".

So many people had promised to do that, and nothing suitable had materialised. But all over the world friends were praying about our need for premises, so something MUST turn up soon.

Sure enough, a duplicated circular arrived a few days later, with a large cross beside the details of Hallaton Hall, Hallaton, Leicestershire, the home of the "Vocation Sisters". It sounded a possibility; forty rooms, nine acres of ground, derelict coach houses—it was worth looking at anyhow!

The weather on the 17th October 1973 was very unsettled. We travelled through torrential rain and thunder to visit Hallaton. We parked the car beside the ruined coach houses and stepped out. The rain had stopped by this time, though large drops were still falling from the huge horse-chestnut tree in the courtyard. The sun shone, making the dripping leaves sparkle. Suddenly, as if pre-arranged, a most wonderful bird-song began. We stood amazed. What a welcome! Then the Mother Superior, Mother Mary Joseph, came out to meet us.

Oh dear! The outside of Hallaton Hall looked most

uninviting! Scarred stonework and rotting window frames, tumble down sheds—our hearts sank! We had visited so many houses which had been lovely old homes in years gone by, but which now were pathetic wrecks. Was this yet another?

We went inside. The house was almost empty, and most of the windows were shuttered—a gloomy start! But as we walked from room to room it was as if the Lord was speaking to us, showing us what He wanted to make of this house.

· "The kitchen is a long way from the dining-room", we said, looking at the antiquated fittings there.

"Oh, we managed!" said the intrepid Mother Superior.

I looked at the long sloping passageway between kitchen and dining-room and had a mental picture of our girls running down it, pushing trolleys laden with hot soup!

"I think *this* room would make a better kitchen,"-said Ron. "It is nearer, and we might manage to have a small lift or something to counter the different levels, in the place of that old range over there."

From that moment it seemed as if everything fitted into place. We began to form a picture in our minds of what we could do to make it "home" for the Torch Family. The interesting thing is, that apart from small details, the picture we had then became a reality!

The large lounge, facing south and overlooking the garden, was very light and pleasant. It had been adapted and used as a chapel by the nuns. The Mother Superior nodded towards two doors at one end of this room. "Those were our confessionals, but you could do what you liked with them." We made no reply, but we could see the family making use of them for telephones eventually.

The winter-garden was the next surprise. Here red and pink geraniums climbed high up the supporting poles, and plumbago hung like a lacy blue umbrella. On two sides, the walls were of specially absorbent rock, with crevices in which plants could be grown. "What a delightful place!" we exclaimed. The atmosphere was so peaceful.

We walked through the winter-garden into a "music-room" There on the wall was a picture of a ploughed field, and the

text: "Except a corn of wheat fall into the ground and die it abideth alone". We stood, looking at the deep clay furrows and thinking of the painful times through which we had passed, not knowing that still more awaited us! We prayed that those ploughing times would not be in vain, but would lead to a harvest that was "a hundred-fold".

Temporarily we had forgotten the Mother Superior. We turned to her, pointed to the picture, and said, "How true!" She nodded—it was a nod of fellowship! She had to leave us then as the Father had arrived to call the nuns to mass. They were living in a small fifteen-room unit, a little to the side of the house.

"Goodbye, and God bless you", Mother Mary Joseph cried as she ran off to mass. "We'll pray that you have this house!"

The family in Sussex were full of questions, and we tried to give them a little picture of the house, which, as I wrote in my diary, had "distinct possibilities".

One of our blind committee members felt constrained to visit Hallaton. We badly wanted to know what a blind person thought about the house. With characteristic thoroughness, John Sharp went over the property three times in minute detail, with the growing conviction that this was to be the family's home.

The auction was coming up on the 11th December. We had no leading as to where we could get any money, and we had only £24,000 in a Development Fund. Hallaton Hall would need that much spent on alterations alone to make it suitable for us! So we decided not to bid at the auction, but asked our friend Sidney Lawrence, who was minister of a church in Leicester, to sit in and inform us as to what happened. He reported that the auctioneer asked for bids for £120,000. There were none. So bidding started at £70,000 and went up to £92,000. The house was then withdrawn as it had not reached its reserve price. At this time there was a tendency for any likely old property to be razed to the ground so that the site could be developed for private housing. There was the mention of developers wanting to buy Hallaton Hall for £100,000. Developers had been our difficulty over several

13

other properties we had looked at. Well, if Hallaton Hall was to be ours, the Lord would see that it did not go to developers! So we left it in our Heavenly Father's Hands.

It was very hard to wait! We were living in daily frustration because of the shortage of room at Hurstpierpoint, so that the waiting was aggravated. Every time we had to make purchases, or decide about where to put staff, we seemed to say the same old thing: "Well, of course, when we move . . ." The very strain of living like this nearly caused us to rush ahead of God's leading. We heard from the agent that there were other interested parties, but that if we liked to make an offer approaching £100,000 it might be accepted. We phoned round the Committee members immediately, and eventually fixed on the price of £90,000. Next day we had a £1,000 gift ear-marked for the new building, so we felt increasing confidence to go ahead. We decided to offer £90,000 to the agents. Normally our dear Chairman, Mr. Gladstone Moore, would have handled the matter, but he was in hospital and, somehow, that offer was never passed on to the vendor's agent. The Lord has wonderful ways of over-ruling our hasty human decisions, when He knows that we truly want His will.

Meanwhile, we arranged to take all the Committee up to see the house. So, at the end of January 1974, several visits were paid to Hallaton as the Committee's inspections began.

I went with Rona, pacing out the rooms, seeing the lovely carved fireplaces and the solid oak panels. I pointed out the air-raid shelters which, in my mind's eye, were already housing our tape and talking book equipment. Rona was enthusiastic! We walked upstairs, looked at both floors, and saw the possibilities there too. Meanwhile the rest of the party was solemnly walking through the rooms. The back parts of the house were especially derelict—I had already planned a super little flat there, but the realists among us looked at it as it was, rather dark and dingy, even damp in places, and altogether the wrong shape. Talk about two men looking through prison bars—one group saw mud, the other, stars! Oh well, it was necessary. We had to weigh up the cost and know for sure that it was God's Will. In this we were all one. To know the Will of God was the main point of our prayers. One of the Committee, a skilled 'do-it-yourself' enthusiast, was quite impressed. He could see that the basic structure of the house was solid and good; it was the later additions which were poor. Electric wiring had been trailed haphazardly to suit the previous owners. Some of the wires looked as if they had been knitted, they were so intertwined! However, the basic original wiring was very good indeed.

With us on this occasion were a couple who had offered their services to us at the Filey Holiday Crusade 1973. Wally and Freda Tobutt were certainly sent to help us at the right time! Wally surveyed the ruins that day, the rubbish lying around, the repairs which needed to be done, and the generally sad state of the decor. He and Freda were not put off at all. They wrote to us the next day, mentioning the experiences of Nehemiah the prophet, who rebuilt ruined Jerusalem. "We are of a mind to work! Nehemiah found the walls broken down, we have found them strong and sound, but there is much 'rubbish to be cleared'. I doubt whether we will need to arm anyone with sword, spear or bow, but if anyone likes to borrow a saw, hammer or pair of pincers, I shall be most happy to oblige!" We laughed; Wally's comparison was very apt. There was much rubbish around to be sure!

So, although that bleak, cold January day seemed disastrous with regard to the approval of the Committee, there were some who caught the vision. Soon the others began to see the potential of the place. The main difficulty in some of our dear Committee's minds was that it would mean moving from the south-east to these northern wilds, thus separating us from our many local helpers. We saw this too, and felt it keenly. But we could also feel the pressure of the Hand of God to move us to a more central position which would be such a help in reaching the growing number of Fellowship Groups.

All of us felt the responsibility of making a right decision. The matter was discussed and prayed over, both individually and at Committee meetings, as we asked the Lord to guide us. We felt we needed some other touch to confirm the Lord's leading. Then we heard from the agent that the specification for the Hall had been altered. Instead of the Hall, coach houses and nine acres for £100,000, we were offered the Hall, coach houses and four-and-a-half acres of land for £50,000, and the out-buildings together with the fifteen-bedroom block which the nuns now occupied, for £20,000. The remaining land with a small bungalow, the vendors proposed to hold, in the hope of obtaining planning permission for development later on.

This was wonderful! We had already had to face the fact that our family was too big to fit into the Hall alone. We should have needed to build an office immediately and look around for bedroom accommodation too. Hallaton Hall had plenty of room for development, but it was costly enough to buy, without having to build straight away. We should be very glad of the fifteen bedrooms in that extra block! In fact, the more we thought about it, the more we saw the Hand of God in this change of specification. We noticed another miracle-touch when we realised that we should not have to apply to a local council for "change of use", as the nuns had been using the premises for printing, personal work, worship and the equivalent of houseparties. Where else could we have found premises with such similar previous use?

Around this time we had the offer of a large interest-free

bridging loan to carry us over the period between moving from Hurstpierpoint to Hallaton, and selling the smaller property. Eventually, at the end of May 1974, negotiations started. The nuns were co-operative all the way through and wanted to help us in every way possible. They were anxious about leaving a bungalow, which was on the land not included in the sale, without an inhabitant. They asked us if we could put someone in this bungalow to care-take. They also asked us if we could look after the lower field which was part of the land which they were holding. This meant that we had the use of the whole of the grounds and of the bungalow, St. Gemma's, on condition that we would take care of them. This was a tremendous help to us for the first year.

Then wonderful little signs were given to us here and there. Of course, we needed an architect. So many jobs required expert advice. Planning authorities and fire precaution people had to be satisfied—yes, we needed an architect all right!

We phoned our friend Sidney Lawrence again to see if he could recommend an architect. He and his congregation had just built a splendid church and we thought he might have recent knowledge about such things. But it was not the architect who planned the church who was in God's Mind for us. In that church a couple had recently been brought to the Lord at their daughter's baptism. They themselves asked to be baptised. "Dad, what are you going to do for the Lord?" asked the keen young daughter. Dad was a little puzzled. He had no idea! All he could offer was the fact that he was an architect! That very evening Sidney Lawrence asked him if he would recommend an architect for some friends of his who were moving up to Hallaton. Eventually we met, and have had very lovely fellowship with Alistair and Delia Reid ever since. Alistair offered his services free—for Christ's sake!

The heating of the house posed a big problem. It had been partially warmed by antiquated night storage heaters that just ate up the current. They had the habit of creaking and groaning in the middle of the night, and only stopped if the would-be sleepers hit them in the middle! Long ago, when we first started to help blind people, one of the girls was badly burned by an electric fire in her bedroom in a hostel to which we had sent her. We felt very strongly that open electric fires were *out!* We were not too keen on convectors either; they too could be a danger if misused. So what were we to do about central heating for this enormous place? It would obviously cost many thousands to have an adequate service installed. And the plumbing! The hot water system was amusing; the minute you turned on the cold tap, the hot tap would stop running. There was very little good plumbing in the house at all.

Here again, God had prepared His own answer to our need. We asked our friend Brian Whiteside for advice as to the best method of heating the house. He told us that he had met a young Christian plumber who was very interested in offering his services to us. David Ballantyne had previously worked on the heating for the small hut at Hurstpierpoint, and had done several other jobs for us there. He had followed our move with prayerful interest, and now came forward to dedicate himself to God to tackle the great task of putting in a hot and cold water system and central heating. He offered to work as a missionary-member of our staff until the job was completed. It was a real step of faith for David and Frances, his fiancée, as they planned to be married early the next year! David has installed one-and-a-quarter miles of pipes, and has given us an efficient hot water supply and a warm cosy home. It took a long time, as you can imagine, and meanwhile we had to live and work in the house. Two mild winters eased the situation while this work was being completed, and we felt how good it was of the Lord to help us in this way. How we appreciated it when, at last, the hot taps really worked, and tepid baths were inconveniences of the past!

But a task so complex as supplying a hot water system and central heating to a house the size of Hallaton Hall required an expert to plan the system. Brian Whiteside, who had put us in touch with David, spent many hours calculating the most economical type of heating, and planning the maze of pipes, the electrical circuits, the boiler room, the storage tanks and the best types of radiators.

What a thrill it is to belong to the same Family, to be members of the same spiritual Body! We were touched again and again by the wonder of it, as people in all walks of life gave their knowledge and skill to the Lord in this sacrificial way!

But in the July of 1974 we could not see as far as the installation of the central heating. I shall never forget the chilling effect of a meeting which was held in Hallaton at that time. Wally was there, ready to get on with the work. Several friends from Leicester had come too. The architect, still a very new Christian, wanted to know how much money we could spend on getting the house habitable. We, of course, had nothing at all, for our savings would have to go towards buying the property.

"No money?" he asked incredulously.

"No", we replied. "Nothing but a very rich Father!"

It was a new experience for our architect friend, but as he followed subsequent events, his faith in God was strengthened.

But the group meeting that day in July could only see a house badly in need of repairs, with non-existent money! Some folk were terribly pessimistic. I remember feeling like a corked-up ginger-beer bottle! I wanted to explode and say, "I *know* God will do it! He has brought us here". These dear folk had never met us before; they had not been to Hurstpierpoint, so they thought that we were, to put it mildly, rather over-ambitious about the whole thing.

"Well", said Ron at length, "we expect to use this house in November for a conference of seventy people".

"You mean November next year", they said.

"No, I mean *this* November", said Ron firmly.

They nearly fainted! They were too polite to say that we were mad, though I am sure some of them thought it! They told us it was an impossible target and highly dangerous for us to think of bringing blind people into an unfinished house. They did not know the restricted conditions in which we were working, nor the urgency of our need, which forced us to press on. The conference in November would have to take place at Hallaton, because there was absolutely no room for it at

Hurstpierpoint. Although I couldn't explain it to these dear, earnest, solemn men, I knew Ron was right. With God all things are possible.

. . . That conference *did* take place!

Our plans for the house must have sounded very hazy to our friends, though they were daily becoming clearer to us. Most of the members of that first working committee stayed with us, and they rejoiced in the wonderful ways in which God guided and provided.

It was at this time that we realised that Hallaton Hall had once been the home of the famous cricketer-missionary, C. T. Studd. He spent his boyhood years in the village of Hallaton, and it was here at the Hall that his father reared some of his famous race horses.

Then we needed a builder. He came on a day when Ron was out, so I had to explain the suggested alterations to him. Sometimes people with whom I had shared my ideas had considered me a visionary, and not a very practical one either! But from the first, this builder treated me as if I knew what I was doing! I showed him the dirty, dark larders and the shed.

"I want this to be a flat", I said. I explained my ideas.

"Ah, yes", he said, "that's quite feasible!"

We went round the house together. Sometimes he suggested small alterations to save a little money. But everywhere he saw the potential and what we really needed. He fell in love with the old house, and captured the spirit of it as he altered it for our needs. Of course, there was the little problem of payment. We told him openly that we had no funds, but he didn't flinch. And we were able to meet all his bills, even though they amounted to more than £20,000 over the first year.

Our builder enabled us to obtain the gift of a swimming-pool presented by Messrs. Corah Bros. of Leicester. It is a small circular pool, just large enough to have a good splash in! The builder fitted it for us free of charge. In the lovely warm summer which followed, the staff and visitors were very glad to use the pool.

Then it was as if a canvas unrolled before us, studded with

miracles of all kinds. There was the army of helpers who came forward: Malcolm, Ben, Matt, Hilda, Hugh, Ray, and a group of volunteers from the locality who rallied to the tasks which needed to be done. Each visit we paid to Hallaton from Hurstpierpoint was an exciting revelation as we saw new progress being made. Several churches in Leicester and Thrapston sent teams of young people to help us. Some were wonderful and helped us enormously; others didn't manage quite so well—but there, that is life!

When we brought some of our blind family to see the house, their reactions were not so enthusiastic. It seemed to be so big, and the echo of feet on the wooden floors nearly sent them crazy! We realised how much people without sight depend on the right type of echo. We also discovered that we should have to carpet the stairs and main floors to reduce the noise-level which was confusing. So we called in our friend Graham to ask his advice.

"My!" he said, scratching his head as he looked at the fifty-foot lounge. "I'll have to quote you by the acre here!"

He and his firm, Erreys of Heathfield, gave us an extremely good quote and advised us as to the best carpet for each room. It was a thrill when the time came for the carpets to be laid! The echo was reduced immediately, and has been no more trouble to anyone.

Curtains! We had nothing long enough to cover the fifteen-foot high windows in the principal rooms. Then one of our lovely Fellowship Group leaders came to see us, complete with lists and colour charts for ready-made curtains, and materials by the yard. We chose bright colours, red and purple in the main lounge to brighten up an oatmeal carpet, and yellow and orange in the dining-room to contrast with the dark panelling. Only long afterwards, when all our orders were delivered, did we know that all this curtaining which we had chosen had been given to us! One of our daughters came along just then and helped us to make the material up into curtains. At last they were hung, and the place began to look like home!

Our next help came from an open prison not far away. A small team of prisoners, usually three or four men, came each

Saturday to work voluntarily in the garden and in the house. Immediately they started to make an improvement as they tidied up the overgrown paths, helped to erect shelves in the production department, renewed plaster, and even made and fitted some new window frames.

The climax of our preparations came as we prepared for Opening Day in June 1975. We worked extra hard for weeks in our struggle to tidy up the garden and house. From all over the country, folk kept writing to say that they were coming, and we realised that we could expect a crowd! We hadn't anticipated that so many would be interested. We had not actually completed our move up from Hurstpierpoint by this time either. There were still items of furniture and furnishings down there. How could we manage to cope with such a large number? How could we show them round, and how could we feed them? And oh, what should we do with the garden, which was still very overgrown in places?

We needn't have worried! The Lord was in full control. The prison authorities found that their craft instructors were having a holiday, and they wanted to know if we could employ some of the prisoners for a week. So, just before Opening Day, we had a team of fifteen working full-time, clearing the garden and making it look really beautiful! Then the friends from the churches around banded together and took over the task of providing teas, hot dogs, ices and sweets arranged on stalls round the lawn. They also provided guides and messengers, car-park attendants, and the like. It was an inspiration to see the way young and old came to help us.

Then there was the miracle of the flies! Every day that early summer we had been bothered by swarms of flies all over the lawn, partly due to the fact that the undergrowth had been unchecked for so long. The swifts would fly over the lawn constantly, swooping down and eating some of these flies; you could hear the sharp click of their beaks as they closed over the prey. The swarms of flies seemed as dense as ever. As the men mowed the lawn, they were harassed by the flies to the point of distraction, yet we were planning to have a meeting outside, sitting on those lawns! Imagine the fidgeting, the scratching, the waving of programmes, the discomfort . . . ! As a family, we prayed that the Lord would take the flies away for the time of our meeting. AND HE DID! The flies were there on Friday, they were there on Sunday, but the air was clear on Saturday! We all knew that this was not coincidence, but the finger of God. How we praised Him that day! Here we were, in our lovely home, with so many blessings from the Lord! We couldn't help but think that C. T. Studd would have been happy to have seen his childhood home so used in the service of the Lord.

One little sadness crept into the proceedings, for our dear Grandad, beloved by so many at Hurstpierpoint, passed into the Lord's presence two days before Opening Day. He would have been so excited to see how well everything had gone. Perhaps he did!

PRAYER OF DEDICATION

Used at the Torch House Opening Day on 28th June 1975.

"Jesus said to the disciples of John the Baptist: 'Go and tell John what you hear and see: the blind recover their sight, the lame walk, the lepers are made clean, the dead are raised to life, the poor are hearing the Good News—and happy is the man who does not find Me a stumbling block'."

(Matthew 11:4-6)

PRAYER

To the glory of God the Father, Who loved us and made us
   accepted in the Beloved;
To the glory of God the Son, Who loved us and gave Himself
   for us;
And to the glory of the Holy Spirit, Who illumines and sanctifies
   us;
We dedicate this house.

For the worship of God in praise and prayer;
For the publishing of His Holy Word;
For the declaration of the Gospel of Jesus Christ, crucified, risen
   and exalted;
For the enlightenment of those who cannot see;
We dedicate this house.

For the giving of light to those who seek the way;
Of strength to those who are tempted;
Of comfort to those who are distressed;
Of support to those who are handicapped;
We dedicate this house.

For the increase of knowledge and the fear of the Lord;
For the teaching and guiding of young and old;
For the recalling of all who stray;
For the up-building of all who believe;
We dedicate this house.

And now we dedicate ourselves, as a fellowship within the
household of God:

   In the unity of the faith,
   In the communion of saints,
   In love and goodwill to all,
   In gratitude for the gift of this house to be a habitation of God
      through the Spirit:
   We dedicate ourselves to the love and service of God and of
      His Kingdom.

Bishop T.S. Garrett, Rector of Hallaton.

CHAPTER 3 — THE FAMILY MOVES IN

It is strange how different a place looks when, at last, it is really your own property. During the negotiations for Hallaton, we could see its potential so clearly that we turned a blind eye to the "black spots". But when we started to take possession, it seemed that everywhere we looked we saw chaos, difficulty, and jobs badly needing to be done.

However, this whole undertaking was God's, not ours. It was too big for us to handle anyway. If He could create beauty and order out of chaos in the universe, it was a light thing for Him to help us!

Wally and Freda quickly settled in, and we realised their sterling worth more and more. In true pioneer spirit they tackled the work, laughing at the difficulties. What happy times we had in the room which is now a laundry, but which they used as a kitchen–dining-room! How we laughed at the 'finds' which Wally and David discovered! An old King George the Fifth coronation flag had been stuffed into a pipe hole in the wall! Old beer bottles from the 1870's were found in the cellars, and other left-overs showed the many different ways in which the house had been used. Margaret McKinstrie was one of the early "settlers". She temporarily took over the work of the laundry and decided to use the bathroom in the main house for the washing. It was a familiar sight to see Margaret kneeling on the landing before her little spin-dryer with clothes-horses round her, as the bathroom was not big enough for the complete operation.

The phone was a vital link between Hurstpierpoint and Hallaton. However, the phone at Hallaton was near the winter-garden and right away from the part of the house occupied by the few pioneers. It was difficult enough to *hear* the phone bell, but it was even more difficult to reach the phone in time, as invariably the caller had given up all hope of a reply by the time the Hallaton folks could reach the instrument. Freda, resourceful as ever, solved the problem by jumping on her bicycle and speeding down the long, sloping passage—until Wally banned it as too dangerous!

Regional Conference—that November conference already referred to—was makeshift in nature. We used oddments of furniture, zed-beds and mattresses, we borrowed blankets, and hung anything available at the windows as temporary curtains. Most of the family was still at Hustpierpoint, so the cooks there could not spare much of the cooking equipment. This limited the menus and called for great resourcefulness. The girls managed well. They balanced a large pan of porridge on a tiny trolley and then had to wheel it from laundry-room (cum-kitchen) to dining-room. Yet with all the improvisations, we were kept from accidents and the conference was a very profitable one. And how we enjoyed sitting in the entrance lounge, warming ourselves by a cosy log fire, and having fellowship with each other in our new home!

It did show some of the weaknesses in the services of the house, however. The kitchen sinks were still not connected to the main drains, and so buckets were placed underneath which had to be emptied at frequent intervals. The electric fuses blew, and the overflow from a wash-basin on the second-floor found its way through the ceiling and poured on to the landing below. Orange bowls of the cheap plastic variety were used to facilitate our washing arrangements. But it was fun, because we knew that the folk from the regions would pray for us all the more! And in a way, it was *their* house too, the home of the family.

After the Regional Conference, we began the task of moving up in earnest. Oh dear! We had no notion of how much there was to move, nor how involved an operation it would be. Praise God that Hurstpierpoint did not sell quickly!

Tony Gibb soon became the brains behind the move. He seemed to be exceptionally gifted at assessing the cubic space required for each item to be shipped up. A friend gave us an old Ford Thames van which had been used to deliver milk; it still had "Home Farm Dairies" painted on it. The kind friend who had given it, provided it with new tyres and saw it safely through its M.O.T. Test. During the next twelve months, from September 1974, Tony nursed that van like a sick child. It covered 15,000 miles travelling mostly between Hurstpierpoint and Hallaton. It broke down often, and many never-to-be-forgotten journeys were made in it. This van had an excellent ventilation system; there was no fear of the driver going to sleep, but every chance that he would freeze! The weather throughout the winter 1974–1975 was mild however, and the journeys were free from many of the usual hazards of winter travel. That little van saved us from having to call on the services of professional removers, and it also enabled us to tackle the move gradually. Staff were moved up to Hallaton a few at a time. This meant we could spend time with the new arrivals, making sure they could find their way around, rather than having to show the whole family all at once.

We aimed to keep the work flowing without much interruption, and so we decided to move each department separately, with staff and their furniture, knives, forks, beds and clothing. The office was the first department to arrive, just before Christmas 1974.

Tony found that he could take only one wardrobe at a time in the van, so he fitted other items inside it. He filled drawers with boxes and small sundry items tucked in the corners, making full use of the space. This explained the mystery of some urgently-required stationery which was missing. It turned up weeks later—inside the fridge!

Personal effects caused a few headaches. Gemma's rubber plant had grown to healthy, large proportions, but it posed a problem as it was too big to be held by the passenger. It was lodged, sideways on, behind the driver eventually, and managed to survive unharmed. Then there was the adventurous terrapin. It was put in a big washing-up bowl and travelled on the lap of the passenger. There was some concern and disturbance when the terrapin succeeded in getting out and exploring the van!

The Christmas tree was a tradition; it had come from House Number Three and had grown quite large. It must go up to Hallaton! Unfortunately, Tony's mind was busy on more important matters, and the van was just driving off when someone noticed the tree still sitting in the forecourt, waiting! Somehow it was added to the load, and reached its destination, to survive the decorations of two Christmasses before it eventually died.

The biggest consideration as we moved was, of course, the continuity of the work, but we were also praying a lot for the people involved. A number of them were already very insecure, and this move was an enormous problem to them. It was comforting to know that people all over the world were praying for this aspect of the move too. One nightmare journey was undertaken by Tony with someone who was extremely disturbed. We saw him off with very deep prayer for protection, and not only from the traffic, for anything could have happened in the van that day. But Tony was conscious of the supreme power and peace which the Lord gives in such circumstances! The journey up to Hallaton was slower sometimes, as some folk needed to stop more frequently at toilets and service stations. Tony tucked one of the family into the passengers's seat one cold, frosty morning. He wrapped the blankets round carefully, as the van did not have the luxury of a heater of course! At 6.30 a.m. they were ready, passenger tucked up cosily. But after only about twelve miles, a little voice said, "Tony, can you find me . . ."!

Although that van looked as if it was falling to pieces, yet it still pressed on. It had a puncture on the motorway when the friend who gave it was driving. He had to leave a blind boy perched in the van and get under it, with rain pouring down and lorries spraying him with dirty water. But the wheel was changed and all was well. His wife had already told him he needed a new jacket. He believed her after that experience! Only once did the van fail to arrive on schedule. It just stuck in gear at a roundabout and nothing would budge it! Eventually, after even the AA had given up, it was attacked underneath with a crowbar, and the wheels turned again! The brakes gave out another time just as the van drew up in the courtyard at Hallaton.

The most precious load to travel up the M1 in the van was undoubtedly the Braille library. It was a blustery, rainy day when the library was moved, so to prevent rain damage Tony backed the van to the library door at Hurstpierpoint. He could just get his finger between the van and the house wall—there wasn't an inch to spare! Braille books have to be handled carefully so that the braille is not pressed, and this posed quite a problem when they were being packed into the van. Higher and higher the pile of books grew. Tony and Eileen, the librarian, wondered if they would all be able to be fitted in, but yes, the van was filled to capacity when the last book was put into place. Library books pass in and out of the library all the time. Sometimes more volumes are "in" than others, but the move took place when just the right number of books were in—to the very last one! Tony felt the weight of responsibility on that journey. In most cases, those books were the only copies in braille in the world, laboriously transcribed by hand. So keenly did he feel his responsibility that he would not leave the van at all during that journey—not that anyone would be likely to run away with a load of braille, but just because he was so aware of the priceless nature of his load!

These simple, trivial events were a blessing and encouragement to us all as we plodded on with the move. We surely knew that the Director of Operations was the Lord!

At last the dear old van gave up the struggle, and died just before its M.O.T. Test was due. Even then it limped to a scrap yard and was sold for £15! We had two loads left to be shipped up. Our dear friend who gave us the van borrowed a horse-box, and our last two loads travelled in that. The move had taken thirteen months, but because it could be tackled gradually, it was accomplished smoothly and without breakage. What is more, the departments were able to keep functioning all the time.

The heavy machinery was moved professionally with great efficiency. The press, which is a Heidelberg printing machine adapted for producing braille, the electric brailler and the electronic plating machine, were all prepared for removal on the Tuesday. On the Wednesday they were loaded on to the transporter; by Thursday evening they were in place at Hallaton and actually producing our overseas magazine "Link"! One of our good friends used his low loader to move our mobile home up to Hallaton; he also did one journey with the loader stacked with piano, large wardrobes, settees and big chairs. It rained that day, but the furniture arrived in good condition.

Two journeys were also undertaken by our friends from Bethel Church in Wigston. They came to our aid with full-size pantechnicon called "Dorcas". The first journey which

"Dorcas" made for us was eventful. She broke down in the middle of the night at Coulsdon with something wrong with the battery. Tony was awakened at 2 a.m. and went off to the rescue. This involved an exchange of batteries, and a problem ride home for Tony in his own car, with a large battery preventing his bonnet from closing—but all was well in the end!

The forecourt at Hurstpierpoint looked like an auction room that day, as the furniture was brought out to be loaded up. The house was getting very empty now, and beginning to echo as furniture and furnishings were cleared from the rooms. When the bigger kitchen equipment was put on to "Dorcas", the fact that we were moving began to hit us. The potato peeler, deep-fat fryer, refrigerator and large cooker were all loaded up. Then, just at the right moment, a delivery van came down the drive bringing a dish-washer which we had ordered (through Green Shield Stamps) some months before. It would have been too big to have fitted into smaller loads, and here, just as "Dorcas" was waiting, it turned up! There were cheers and praises to God over yet another little miracle.

The minister of Bethel, Rev. Harry Sutton, drove "Dorcas" himself. He loaded her the same day, travelled to Hallaton, unloaded late at night, and returned to base ready to take the Sunday services next day.

Our move taught us a number of lessons. We learned to work as a team, appreciating each other's worth when we were separated, and proving loyalty and love amongst each other. It also showed us the sterling qualities, the self-sacrifice and love of our new neighbours in Leicestershire.

* * * * * *

The family move involved other smaller moves too. Sue and John Oldham joined the staff as soon as we started to move in. They bought a cottage in the village which needed a great deal of attention before it was habitable. They worked long hours, renewing, repairing and re-organising the cottage, and yet never once did they let their work for the Lord take second place. There was enough work to be done on the house to keep them busy for years to come. We are glad they are near enough to share their family with us too!

Eileen Cole and her mother were expert at moving, having had three moves within about two years! At first, while negotiations were in progress for the purchase of a property at Hallaton, Mrs. Cole lived in one room in the "Hall", now re-named "Torch House", and often that room was turned upside down because David was laying pipes under the floor-boards. But, in spite of it all, Mrs. Cole was unperturbed, and even became our ambassador to the village. She would go out for walks and meet the local people, and she did a great deal to help the village accept us as a family. Eventually, she and Eileen moved to the "Cole Cott", a very pleasant thatched cottage where we are always sure of a welcome at any time. On the whole, accommodation for staff families is a real problem, as very little property is for sale or to rent in the village.

And where should we live? As "Mum and Dad" of the family we felt it necessary to be available, so we converted rooms to make a flat on the first floor of the main house. It was an exciting experience setting up home again after six years at Hurstpierpoint, during which time our own home had been absorbed into Torch. The Lord gave us such a lot more than we had given Him, and we found ourselves with a beautiful lounge-dining-room, a bedroom, bathroom, and a super modern kitchen with the latest Schreiber fitments, cooker and refrigerator —all a gift from His own loving Hand. It was certainly a thrill to do a little cooking and to make a dinner for our own children when they visited us. We also found the privacy of the flat helpful when we had problems to discuss, leaders' meetings, and people in need of prayer and love. And of course, when we managed to get time off, it was wonderful to have a little spot in which to relax.

By summer 1975 the bulk of the move was over. The family was settling into the village happily, and we felt that we had really "come home".

CHAPTER 4 — LIVING TOGETHER

It was a December Sunday morning soon after we had completed our move. Logs crackled and flared in the old fireplace in the entrance lounge as the family gathered round for a time of open Bible study, which in those days we used to have after the Communion Service. They sat on the carpet mostly, though some were on chairs or on the arms of chairs. Print Bibles of all versions were in evidence, and braille volumes of the Acts of the Apostles, for that day the subject under discussion was the Holy Spirit. We had been thinking about the Holy Spirit for some weeks, and had traced His work in the Old Testament, then in the life of the Lord Jesus, and were now considering His ministry in the early church. Our young folk always came straight to the point, and it was not long before somebody said, "What is the 'Baptism of the Spirit?' Is this what we are reading about here?"

Her finger was resting on the dots in the braille volume. There was a slightly awkward silence. She had brought us straight into an area of controversy. We looked round the room. Some of the folk had been greatly blessed by their experience in the Holy Spirit, but a number of the young people were very muddled about the subject. Others still smarted under the memory of sad divisions and disruptions, which had been caused by dogmatic assertions as to these experiences in their home churches. Many fellowships have floundered on these rocks; how could we have a friendly discussion on such a thorny subject?

One of our visitors, a well-loved friend of the family, almost imperceptibly took the lead. He had no braille Bible available, and the print versions were useless to him as he could not see. But that was no handicap to him as the Word was stored firmly in his heart. Some of the young folk began to talk eagerly about their experiences "in the Spirit". One, straining forward in her chair and peering up from her large print Bible, which was open at 1 Corinthians 12, told us how the gift of tongues had helped her. A braille reader said, "But surely not everyone has to speak in tongues. I don't."

From the other side of the room a sighted member of the family, who had had quite a lot of experience in leading young people's groups, shared that this insistence on everyone "speaking in tongues" had caused a deep split in his youth group and church. A blind girl spoke up; she was a keen Bible student and had a wonderful knowledge of the Scriptures. She shared how the gift of speaking in tongues had helped her in her private devotions. Then she went on to say, "I think a lot of churches are put off from enjoying the gifts of the Spirit by the devil, who is using unhappy divisions to scare people away from all forms of spiritual gifts."

Gently our leader encouraged those from each school of thought to air their views. We became aware of the precious privilege we were enjoying. How thankful we should be that such a frank discussion could be carried on in such a loving atmosphere! Everyone had an opportunity to speak, and most people did join in. Yet no one became heated, or hurt, and we all learned from each other.

"Well", said one of our number who might have been labelled pentecostal by some, "I'd like to say what a blessing it has been to me to hear you folks who don't go in for a great show of spiritual gifts. I've especially appreciated the way you have shared those Bible verses with us—they were great!"

"For my part", said one of our lady workers, who had suffered a lot in the past over this subject, "I want to thank you folks who are a bit charismatic, for the way you haven't rammed it down our throats. I can see that the Holy Spirit is really helping you. You have shown it in your lives".

We ended the session with a lovely time of open prayer, asking that the Lord would continue to teach us more about Himself through His Word.

Over the years, our Sunday morning pattern has changed, and we spend much longer in worship and praise, reserving our main times of Bible study and discussion for Wednesday evenings.

Because staff and visitors came from such different backgrounds, we faced a problem when we were considering the pattern for our worship. Take Communion for example: some preferred individual cups, some one cup, some felt at home with a pastor leading the meeting, others were used to varying degrees of freedom in worship. Some liked the reverence of quiet formality; others liked to express their worship in a more spontaneous way!

The Lord has done a wonderful thing over the years in moulding our times of Communion. There is not a rigid order of procedure; it can vary slightly from week to week, but always it is a sweet, precious time of drawing close to our dear Saviour. We sing well-loved hymns and choruses, so full of meaning; we have quiet too, when we can silently express our love to the Lord. We have a period of open worship when we share, out of the fulness of our hearts, something of what the Lord Jesus means to us. Usually one of our men folk leads the service, but any may feel free to pray, choose a hymn, pass on to us a thought from the Word of God, or share anything which has moved them to worship. The whole service of Communion may take less than an hour on some occasions; on others it may be longer. Time doesn't seem to matter as we share the eternal wonder of the love which brought our Lord to earth to die for us.

As we have so many families belonging to our staff, we have a children's talk at the beginning of our communion time, so that the little ones can worship with us for a few minutes at the start of each service.

Practical details have had to be worked out with a view to our special difficulties. For example, a row of blind people, some of them visitors and unfamiliar with our ways, would find it disturbing and inhibiting to break off a piece of bread from a round loaf on a slippery plate, so we prepare the bread, cutting it into small pieces. We share a common cup. Blind folk find a "retiring" offering an embarrassment, as they cannot easily locate the box, so we have an offering as part of our worship, when bags are passed round. This money goes into a special Communion Fund, to be given to Christian workers at home and overseas. Such practical points as these had to be solved by our family, so that nothing need distract from our worship as we gather in the chapel each Sunday morning at 10.30.

* * * * * *

But we have our natural pleasures too. Come for a Sunday afternoon walk with "Cud"! Make sure you have got your wellington boots on, because "Cud" has the propensity for finding the muddiest walks around! The countryside is laced with footpaths, and full of interest. Fortunately not all the walks are muddy! A circular three-mile favourite takes you to the village of Blaston and back without the need to leave tarmac paths.

Sunday is specially a family day. Some folk sit around by the fire in the entrance lounge, talking. Others listen to records, or read or write letters. In the summer, there are little groups to be seen outside enjoying the gardens. It is refreshing to worship, walk, chat and be together in the consciousness of the Presence of the Lord.

On Sunday evenings we go to different churches to have fellowship with local Christians. Some of these churches have been specially warm in their welcome, and have taken a great interest in particular individuals from our family. This weekly contact is a great help in avoiding spiritual insularity.

* * * * * *

There were groans when we first moved up to Hallaton and discovered that there were only two buses a week! But it is amazing how the family is finding ways of getting around. A trip to Market Harborough is quite an education; a bus ride seems to be a social occasion round here. It was on the bus that we had our first real contact with our neighbours. The ride is delightfully noisy, everyone talking at once. The "fortunates" on the front seat have to control the opening and shutting of the door sometimes. On the return journey the bus can be loaded with prams, dogs, goldfish, boxes, bulging bags, hungry children, and mums and dads of all shapes and sizes. Bargains are bragged about, cheap offers displayed, and of course the latest village gossip is passed on. What a welcome change from the silent isolation of sophisticated travel in some parts of the South-East!

We have had a very warm welcome from the villagers, and have grown very fond of them. The village is built round a green where the old Butter Cross is a meeting-point for the young folk. Thatched cottages with their old pumps look up to a large stately church and rectory. Then, clustered together, are the school, chapel, three pubs and a village shop which sells stamps and bacon, biscuits and brightly-coloured balls, and just about everything else! There is a recreation ground where sheep graze safely, except when a cricket match is in progress. There is a pond too, with the notice, "For the use of local residents only". One of our guide-dogs (obviously intelligent) decided to make use of the local facilities for a bathe—much to the surprise of hundreds of goldfish in the pond who were not used to being "fished for" in such an energetic way! Most of our intrusions into local affairs have been less boisterous. Occasionally, some of the staff have been to badminton, Women's Institute, and a number have joined a house Bible Study which started some while before we moved into the area.

As in all villages there are "outstanding characters". Donald the milkman is one. He is cheerful and good-hearted under all circumstances. Early in the morning, yawning at the wheel of his delivery van, or stooping in the road, retrieving the remains of a milk bottle which has fallen out, he is always the same, and most interested in us and our doings. One day he looked into the car, glanced at the occupants of the back seat, and said, "Those two young ladies . . . are they . . . you know . . . can they see?" The two blind girls in the back of the car giggled. You cannot take offence, because Donald is genuinely interested. He has set himself the task of learning the names of everyone in our large family. It means a lot to people who cannot see to be greeted by name. Well done, Donald! He is most generous too, and often a carton of cream has found its way to the dining-room without coming through expenses.

And for the first four years we enjoyed the services of Kathy! On Thursdays the call went out, "Anyone want a hair-do?" For Kathy came complete with curlers, dryer and scissors, to tidy us up! At first, Kathy used to do her shampooing in very primitive conditions, but later she had a wash-basin in her "salon" in the new bathroom block. I remember the difficulties we had in Sussex when we took our blind family for hair appointments and had to call back for them an hour later. It was good to be helped on the premises by someone as charming as Kathy. When she moved from the village, we were so relieved to have the services of Brenda to take Kathy's place.

Soon after we moved to Hallaton, the doctors who held the village surgery twice a week found themselves "homeless". They tried to get other accommodation, but nothing was forthcoming. We prayed for them, as the village needed to have surgery facilities. The Lord reminded us of our own newly-decorated medical room, and the cosy entrance lounge, an obvious place for the waiting-room. We offered these facilities to the doctors, and they eagerly accepted. So, on Monday and Thursday mornings the village come to us! One of our staff turns receptionist for that brief hour, and is able to have a number of helpful conversations with patients as they wait.

There were practical problems to be worked out when calling people to meals. The gong in the hallway was adequate for the house, but it couldn't be heard in Bethany, the name given to the 15-bedroom block across the courtyard. The only answer was to use the bell which hung high above the back door. So, at five minutes to eight, as each day's programme begins, the bell is rung to call people to breakfast. At eight o'clock the gong sounds in the hall, and sleepy-eyed people begin to make their way to the dining-room. The day has begun.

For the house-staff work has begun before this, as breakfast has to be prepared. Obviously we do not all have a working day of nine to five-thirty. Those who prepare breakfast have time off later in the day. Again, as many visitors call on us on a Saturday, not everyone can have Saturday as a day off. Sometimes too, special jobs make it necessary for folk to work on after tea. Our working hours are governed by the very motive which brought us together, a desire to give our lives in service to the Lord.

The work is more separated now that we have extra space. This is good, as each department is increasing in size, necessitating more staff to cope with the volume of work. So, after the move to Hallaton, it became necessary to alter our former practice of having all the staff together for elevenses. When this change was suggested we met with many protests.

"Oh, don't miss that out! How can we keep together as a family if we miss our mid-morning prayer time?"

There was real consternation and the fear of our becoming an institution. We *so* wanted to stay as a family. Surely, because we were in this lovely big house, and numbered fifty, we need not stop being a family! It was good to take this worry to the Lord. He showed us how big His family was, and that the spirit of caring and sharing, the rule of love, were what made a family. So we took a few practical steps to keep personal contact with each other. We appointed leaders to whom people could go if they found it difficult or impossible to come to us. Jethro's advice to Moses helped us there! Also, we arranged to meet for prayer with each department every two weeks. In this way we were able to keep close contact with those who work in the Production Block, the Tape Department, the Office, the House, the Library and Editorial Departments, and the Maintenance staff. At these gatherings the staff and family could raise any points which worried them, report any broken machinery, any hold-up in the work, and anything at all relating to their department. On Thursdays a full staff-meeting was called, when more general problems could be discussed and prayed over. In this way we tried to foster a spirit of loving concern for each other as we worked together.

Chapel time has become the highlight of our day. After the clatter and the chatter of dinner-time, the swish of the washing-up machine, the drying of cutlery, re-setting of tables, stacking away of crockery—all jobs which are shared throughout the family—it is lovely to be in the quiet peace of the chapel and to relax. Sometimes we come in, harassed by all we have to do, wishing we hadn't got this daily appointment with God. But oh, the refreshment of a short while in His Presence! It really does renew our strength. Chapel time usually starts with a hymn or chorus. Then one of the family, older or younger, passes on a thought from the Bible. Prayer requests selected from the post are shared. Members of the Torch Family in many parts of the world write in and ask us to pray for them. In fact anyone can share a problem or a joy at chapel time. Occasionally letters are read out when they concern the whole family—how often we have been able to rejoice together at answers to prayers offered in the chapel!

* * * * * *

"What shall we do with ourselves in the winter evenings?" said some of our staff when they first arrived. The evenings were quite a concern to us. We were rather too far away from good evening activities to attend them regularly, yet we could do with something to interest and foster our creative talents. So we tried to organise our own "evenings at home". Soon a most ambitious list appeared on the noticeboard, giving a choice of courses which we could run. These gradually began to be sorted out. Some evenings small groups would be busy cooking, and exotic smells would come from the kitchen. Later, contented folk would be sitting in the coffee-bar eating the food which they had cooked. Sometimes, you could walk into the lounge and find bodies lying on the floor, trying to keep fit.

On Tuesday evenings we have choir practice, and it is exciting to see how the Lord is using our choir to serve Him. Then Bible study groups are held on Wednesday evenings in the houses of different members of staff. Some of the folk who come to us have missed a background knowledge of the Scriptures, and have many questions which they are longing to put forward. These smaller groups give them an opportunity for discussion, and they are able to ask any questions they wish. We also have outings, swimming and walks which can fully occupy any spare time we might have. If none of these activities appeal, then people can always chat to members of staff, who are appointed as hosts or hostesses in the lounge each evening.

Christmas is a happy time at Torch House. The house is decorated with greenery from the garden, and the Christmas tree stands in the panelled entrance-lounge dressed with fairy lights. We never cease to be amazed at the goodness of God in providing so much that we would regard as extra to our needs. Each Christmas this provision has come our way, and we have been able to offer our visitors plenty of fruit and nuts, chocolates and sweets.

Come and meet these visitors as they are opening their presents on Christmas morning. This is our oldest guest; she is eighty-four, is blind, and has no relatives at all. I think she finds it all a little bit noisy! She has a lap full of presents. "Such a surprise, my dear! It is so nice to be remembered".

Another blind lady here has recently been widowed, and has lost interest in living. It is good to see her smile as she opens a gaily-wrapped present. Young students from abroad are having fun trying to find their way round this strange house—quite an undertaking, as they are blind. This bright-faced young woman is not only blind but deaf as well. What fun she is having! The staff always feel specially drawn to the deaf-blind who miss so much. Children are around too. In fact there are several of each age-group here, so no-one need be lonely!

The Christmas programme centres round the precious Gift above all gifts, the Lord Jesus. We usually have Communion on Christmas Eve, and a short service on Christmas Day with the children in mind. In the afternoon we have an amateur pantomime which is warmly applauded. Games play a part too. Music from the record-player and also from our own "band" helps to fill the days of holiday with family enjoyment. Any instrument is accepted into that band. We have amateur performances on flageolets, harmonicas, cellos, xylophones, guitars, auto-harps, clarinets and glockenspiel. Percussion is not missed out either, for tambourines are present too.

We certainly have variety! Just as different colours enhance a picture, so different activities blend to make the pattern of life which God has given us. It seems natural somehow to consider His Presence just as real in the height of the hilarious moments as it is in the quiet of the Communion Service. Didn't He say, "Lo, I am with you always"!

There are other occasions which we must share with you. From time to time, before special events or just when we feel the need for them, we have extra times of prayer. These are precious moments when the family comes together to seek the Lord. Each prayer time has its own special character. At some the emphasis might be on worship and praise, cheering our hearts and, we are sure, bringing joy to the Lord. At other times there may be some specific burden on our hearts—a coming houseparty, a financial need, a loved one in deep distress. As we share these burdens with the Lord and with each other, He answers our prayers marvellously, moving our hearts closer together as a family, and teaching us His pattern for our life together.

CHAPTER 5 — THE HOUSE THAT WOULDN'T SELL

By Summer 1976 we had settled happily into the house at Hallaton, and were feeling more and more at home. But month after month, at the Central Committee meeting, there was one problem item always on the agenda. It was, "Sale of Torch House, Hurstpierpoint". During the move, we had been glad that there were no buyers for the property, as this meant that we were able to move to Hallaton more gradually, with no pressure. We had left one family at Hurstpierpoint as "caretakers", but now that we had moved, we needed to sell the house to be able to pay back a £40,000 bridging loan kindly lent us free of interest by Christian friends.

On two occasions there had been hopes of a sale, but each time the buyer had withdrawn. There was another problem too—the family who were kindly caretaking there did not seem to be successful in finding employment, or other accommodation, try as they would!

So, at every Committee meeting, we listened to these dampening facts, and wondered what to do. Secretly several of us on the Committee felt that it would be a pity to sell at all. But we all studiously kept our thoughts strictly to ourselves! We were so insular, too aware of the implications to say boldly what was in our hearts. One thing we did communicate, and that was our longing to know the Will of God in the matter.

"My sheep hear My Voice"—"Call upon Me and I will answer thee"—"Everyone who is of the truth hears My Voice". These Bible verses, and many instances of the Lord speaking, exercised me greatly. There are in a work like Torch, many occasions when decisions need to be made for which there is no specific guidance in the words of Scripture. Yet surely the Lord has promised to guide us continually. Surely guidance is not a haphazard "hit-and-miss" affair!

"Master, speak, Thy servant heareth . . .
I am listening, Lord, for Thee
What hast Thou to say to me."

"Wait on the Lord" is a phrase often used at these times, by those who believe in the Lord Jesus. We decided that we would do that. We would pray and pray, wait and wait, until we had His answer for the way ahead. We had at times experienced a little of what Brother Lawrence calls the "Practice of the Presence of God". In our quiet times with the Lord, or sometimes in a gathering of His children, we had heard that Still, Small Voice which made the Scriptures live, and which gave comfort, correction and—yes—guidance. It was a most holy, precious experience, which we hardly liked to mention to others.

One of the young people whom God had sent to us, had been in deep mental torment. Her mind had seemed to be so twisted and warped by the terrible things she had suffered, that we were, at times, completely lost as we tried to help her. In our extremity, we took to waiting on the Lord more and more. That Still, Small Voice became *so* precious to us. And as we waited, the Lord showed us how to help this needy girl, how to gently probe, when to point to wrong attitudes, when to use the balm to promote healing. That close contact with the Lord which we were compelled to have, proved to be the means of bringing complete mental healing to one regarded as hopeless. In retrospect, we saw that the Lord, in the stillness of our hearts, had taught us the very best in psychology with what is far greater, the power of His Holy Spirit to cleanse, heal and fill those wasted and wild places in this girl's mind.

Yes, we could humbly claim to have heard the Shepherd's Voice. Sometimes, because I could not remember exactly, and because my way of remembering is writing, I had jotted down some of the things the Lord had said. This enabled me to pray over them and to compare them with the standards and teachings of Holy Scripture. One day, I was alone praying, and I felt the Lord urging me to listen, so I was prepared to write. I was reluctant to do this—part of me wanted to dodge the responsibility of receiving any word of knowledge from the Lord. Let someone else have it—I didn't want to be involved! But the Hand of God was on me, and I took a piece of paper praying that nothing in me, or in my circumstances or in the opinion of my friends, or the suggestions of the foe, *nothing* could intrude upon this fellowship with my Lord. And this is what the Lord said to me that day, "Hurstpierpoint is still part of My purpose for you". The Lord also assured me that He would provide a job and accommodation for the caretakers, which was the other problem.

What was I to do? Those who were on the Committee were sensible, practical people, businessmen in fact. They wouldn't think much of a "word of knowledge" like this. So I did nothing, except to share it with one other lady on the Committee.

Committee day came round again. Soon we reached the perennial problem, "Sale of Torch House, Hurstpierpoint". I fidgeted uncomfortably.

"Don't mention anything" cautioned my mind. "You'll be laughed at. You might lead them all astray. After all, £40,000 is involved. Just keep quiet, it's ridiculous to think of keeping it!"

There was an uncomfortable silence as the Committee members studied the agendas. Then my friend leaned forward, "I think you should share that word" she said. I blushed, and felt very wobbly at the knees, then hesitantly I read my note. "Hurstpierpoint is still part of My purpose for you." Then, getting bolder, I read the promise that the caretakers would find accommodation and a job.

There was silence in the Committee room after I had read the note—it seemed to go on for an eternity to me. Then, a sigh of relief seemed to go round the table, for that word had already been knocking at the hearts of others there. We all bowed our heads, and praised the Lord for confirming what we had all felt deep down. We accepted it as His Will, and prayed that He would show us how to work out the details. I felt that my part was over. The rest was up to others in the Committee meeting.

"We must pay back the £40,000 bridging loan, of course". "Yes, I suggest £1,000 a month". I gasped! Why, since we had come up to Hallaton we had been constantly fighting with bills, and only just balancing income and expenditure. A commitment of an extra £1,000 a month was a crazy idea. My faith was at zero. But those dear godly men were sure this was the way, so there and then they stepped out in faith. And what a peace descended on that Committee! I doubt if any of us will ever forget it.

Well, within two weeks, the family living in the Hurstpierpoint house *had* found a job and accommodation, and every month, without fail, the Lord sent an extra £1,000 to meet the repayment of the bridging loan.

What is more, He caused John and Rosina Sharp, with Phung and Karen, their daughters and Christopher, their son, to move in as house-parents, so that they could supervise the re-decorating and re-furnishing of the house.

Not long afterwards, a ninety-four year old lady, who had never heard or understood the Gospel, came to stay for a holiday. During that time she was 'born again'.

This was the first seal on the ministry which the Lord was opening up for that house at Hurstpierpoint, which became known as "Little Torch". Since then the house has seen a variety of events, happy and sad. Wedding receptions, Golden Wedding celebrations, family reunions, quiet days for Fellowship Groups, holiday parties, and individual guests who come for refreshment and holiday. It has also become an oasis of fellowship for students and on one occasion, it became the gate of Heaven when a very tried and troubled young woman came for a while, and after a very joyful, peaceful fortnight, was taken to be with the Lord. The little chapel there is still calmly welcoming to individuals as well as groups. The team in the house is gradually developing a Bible study ministry too, and who knows what the Lord has in store as we

continue to follow His leading.

There is no doubt that in the first instance, "Little Torch" was given to us by the Lord. Its quiet chapel, lovely views and easy access for wheelchairs, were meant to be used by the Torch family, we have no doubt. We are thrilled as we see the ministry of love and caring which is taking place in that house again.

"Oh trust the Lord ye His Saints—there is no want to them that fear Him."

CHAPTER 6 — FAMILY PROBLEMS

"I should just be in my element if I could have a home like yours, for the blind or the deprived, or . . . ." The speaker was a motherly person, who genuinely wanted to help. Her heart was full of romantic desire to serve the Lord. But I wondered if she knew the more difficult side of sharing one's home with misfits and "nobody's children". Did she know what was entailed when living with such people? Could she imagine their fear and insecurity, psychiatric disorders, and even attempts at suicide? I wanted to take the star-dust from her eyes, to show her a little of the cost, lack of privacy, never being sure of your programme, hearing complaints which seemed to stretch into hours, experiencing tensions unknown before. Perhaps it was just as well that I couldn't explain all that. If we had known these things in 1968, would we have established Torch House at all? Maybe not.

Home is all too often a strange place to blind youngsters, for at five years of age, when their education begins, they often have to leave home to go to boarding school. They are fed, transported, taught and in some cases even clothed by the state. Strong ties with parents will stand the strain of such an upheaval. But where the ties with parents are not strong, far too many families do not survive this separation, resulting in young people who are unwanted and even disowned by their parents when they reach school-leaving age. Some young folk become aggressive, destructive and difficult to live with, and open to catch any of the moral diseases of our times.

Any who open their lives and their homes to such a people soon find that the problem is vast. It is impossible to bring lasting healing to such people without God. Let us share with you some of the shattering situations which we experience, and some of the deep lessons which we are learning as we try to give these people security and love.

"I know I'm selfish—everybody rubs it in—self, self, self, they all tell me, but what can I do? It's all so dark, I'm so afraid—I'm not fit to live—I think I must run away—or kill myself, then I shan't be a nuisance to you, nor a plague to myself."

We know enough about the speaker to realise that she is quite capable of carrying out her threats!

Sitting beside one of our adopted daughters during an outburst like that we feel hopelessly inadequate to cope with the situation. At such times the counselling books which we refer to seem to have no parallel to the case we have in hand. Where are those wonderful promises from the Word which we are supposed to claim and pass on? As we try to grope for them, the mind goes blank, and our faith seems to wobble. Where is the power which we have always believed to be available in Christ? In our weakness we cry to the Lord, pleading for wisdom and understanding. Even as we breathe the Name of Jesus, some of the power, the balm, the healing of that precious Name, reaches down to us. Gradually we feel the tension going from us, and confidence and hope returning, and with it a great tenderness.

That blind girl is still sitting beside us, disconsolate and desperate, her hands tight with tension, as if they would clutch at our faith. But now in the Name of Jesus, we have found a refuge. We can't help, but He can. He understands this girl, oh so much better than we do. He, and He alone can help her.

We have seen such situations as this turned to lasting blessing, when we have stopped trying to apply our own wisdom, and have let the wisdom of God flow through us instead. Truly, "Without Me," said the Lord Jesus, "you can do nothing".

Day-to-day irritations sometimes catch us off guard. We

wait on the Lord about big problems, but often fail to pray about the little ones. Material problems can come in waves and almost overwhelm us with physical demands.

"Come quickly, there's water dripping from the electric light in the cloakroom." We go to discover that a toilet is blocked in the room above, another little job! The immersion heater has broken—we go to inspect it and find that, even worse, the tank has a crack in it! Physical ailments come in groups too, as a diary note for one weekend shows: "Cook in bed, W has a bad back, S has a stiff neck, P fell over and sprained ankle, E has 'flu . . . ." But in the midst of all this God was working; the diary note goes on to say:— "Three deaf-blind visitors arrived—Sue came to know the Lord Jesus!"

How easily our immediate response to interruptions can trigger off unwise words and actions! Sometimes I am trying to write a letter which needs a lot of thought. My mind is engrossed in it. Suddenly the door opens, B blusters in: "When are you going to fix my tape recorder, I want it—now!" I feel like retorting: "Go and get lost!" but I know that I must not do that. Instead I must put aside my letter, and try to see the frustration behind B's bluster—not always an easy thing to do. Decisions can be handled carelessly and the wrong answer given when the mind is otherwise occupied. "Mum Heath, P hasn't got up yet. Shall I rake him out or leave him?" We ask ourselves, "Is he ill, or just lazy?" Sometimes no simple "yes" or "no" can give the answer; we have to find out for ourselves. Perhaps even more irritating are the petty things such as, "S has upset H and she is crying". "Why, what did he do?" "He said her clothes were old-fashioned!"

Little troubles take time to deal with, and can make us feel irritable, or careless, so that we miss bigger issues which are involved. "D is sobbing—he has been doing it for a long time—can you come?" You sigh: "What's wrong now!" You find D crumpled up, with an outsize inferiority complex, because he has tried to do a job requiring more sight than he possesses. He has chalked up another failure in his mind. It is so easy to miss the deep-down hurt to an insecure boy which shows in something trivial. Our minds need to be constantly in tune with the Lord, or they get so full of the mundane things of life that they cannot spot the real needs of the people around us.

Sometimes experiences involve the whole family. C was upset. She and her adopted sister in the family had had a happy morning arranging their new bedroom. The new yellow bedspreads looked fine, and could easily be seen by C who had a fair amount of sight. Even S, her room-mate, could see a tiny glow of colour. S had just lost the sight in her "good" eye, and was now almost completely in the dark. So she merited a little extra fuss, and C gave it, helping to arrange the glass ornaments and other nick-nacks beloved by girls, and making the room what it should be—home! But other people interfered, with good reason, no doubt. They spoke warmly to the afflicted S, and just a tiny bit less warmly to C. "You mustn't put the ornaments there, dear, S will knock them over." "No, let her have this drawer, it will be easier for her." Resentment smouldered, "They're getting at me—it's all S, nobody thinks about me!"

The staff were caught up in the routine of the day, and engrossed by it. No-one noticed white-faced, tight-lipped C getting more and more withdrawn. At tea-time a crowd of visitors came—that meant more work, more bustle, more interest too—visitors are very welcome in the family. So it wasn't until bed-time that C was missed. S discovered the fact first. Consternation spread. Mum and Dad Heath were away, which made matters worse. Search parties set out to scour the village and fields, their minds filled with fears. It was hardest of all for those who were waiting at home. The searchers returned—no clue at all. No-one had seen that lonely little figure as it stole away. At length the Police were informed. They were kind, helpful and optimistic. But a chill descended on the household. Each one was holding an inquest into his own lack of observation or tact. Then a senior member of staff who was left in charge called the folk together into the quiet of the chapel. He read from the Word of God, encouraging, comforting, challenging. Then the family picked up the weapon of "all prayer"—somehow it had not been used very effectively before on that evening. They prayed for C that she would be protected from harm. They asked to be forgiven for any carelessness or selfishness which had hurt her. The prayer session did not end there, it leapt into praise and confidence in the Lord.

Meanwhile, C, with her limited vision seriously impaired by the twilight, was walking down the main road. Young men in fast cars slowed down and wolf-whistled, some even stopped, thinking she was after a 'pick-up'. She returned a stony stare to them all. Surely the 'hosts of God' were working on her behalf that night! At last, foot-sore and very tired, she reached a park eight miles away and sank on to a seat. She put her head in her hands. She felt desolate. "No-one cares—they just don't bother about me." A vagrant came along and sat beside her. She edged away. "Don't do that love. It's cold tonight. Here, come and share my sleeping-bag with me." She turned her back on him and again, the 'hosts of light' stood between her and this poor sin-hardened man. He didn't touch her. Then a policeman appeared. "What's up, my dear?" he asked.

"Nothing", she replied, tonelessly.

"That's not true, you know, else why are you on a park bench at midnight—a young lady like you. Have you run away?"

"Yes—they don't care!"

The policeman talked into his transmitter and reported that he had found her. Then the wheels of the law moved. C was soon being welcomed by a relieved, smiling member of staff. "I didn't think you'd bother that much", she said. Bother? He wisely delayed any reprimand. He just assured her of the love of her earthly family, but most of all he shared with her the deep love and concern of her Saviour.

We have spoken of some of the problems which our family cause us, but sometimes they have very real problems to cope with in their own lives. Usually the main area of conflict is with their families. Although these lovely young people have been so desperately hurt, they will often go to great lengths to keep in touch with their families. Yet the families continue to hurt them. So deep is their desire to "belong" that sometimes young people will invent elaborate stories of imaginary parents and brothers and sisters.

I shall never forget B's sad little face as each morning, in the weeks before Christmas, he felt along the post table to see if there was a letter for him. Eventually, after Christmas, an envelope arrived. It contained a pound note from his family, nothing more. B commented: "Oh, if only it could have been a letter!"

The desire to keep in touch with families has sometimes brought real distress to the young people when they have re-visited their homes. Some of them have partially overcome this problem by taking friends with them. Others have returned to us distressed, and in need of lots of love and extra care for some time. But their families do matter to them, and these young people are anxious to tell their families about the Lord Jesus too.

W introduced us to a new problem. She was a member of a large family, had no job, but received her weekly Social Security from the State. This money was always taken from her by her mother, ostensibly for the family needs, but actually it went on drinks and bingo. W was becoming nervously ill, so we were asked to give her a home, on the advice of her doctor. She came to us, and on the whole settled happily and well. But oh, the pull of that family; they did not want her, no, they soon used her bed, and shared out the few possessions she had left behind at home. But they did want her money! Month after month they begged her to send them money and told her she was no Christian if she didn't help them, and that she was causing them real hardship by living at Torch. She was constantly worried by their convincing arguments. Although she could not see to read, she knew the text, "Honour your father and mother"—perhaps she was not honouring them! W's father had a job, but repeatedly absented himself from it, and both parents were eaten up with their gambling. Inspite of efforts by local Christians, the home situation did not improve. It was hard for W to understand that to give in and send money to her parents from her mere pittance, was not in fact honouring them, but rather encouraging them in their profligacy and neglect of other younger members of the family.

These are just a few of the difficulties with which some of the young members of our family have to come to terms. Some of them dread going to stay with happy families, and Family Houseparties cause such pain that at those times we try to arrange for them to visit friends.

Problems, great and small, are part of life, especially when you are living with needy people. The most devastating mistake when helping such people would be to give up when they become too wearing. That would only add another deep wound to their already scarred lives, and would cancel out all the good which might have already been done. It is because of this fact, and the drain which such people make upon those ministering to them, that we like to share the task of helping and loving them between us. Even so, without the strength and resources of the Lord, we should fail miserably.

Praise God, quite a number referred to in this chapter have become more stable, and are now either serving the Lord elsewhere or valued members of our staff. Just a few still seem to be finding life difficult to cope with.

Problems are a part, but only a part of family life. There are so many compensations, and much joy and laughter too, as we share in the next chapter!

CHAPTER 7 — FAMILY FUN

Every family has its fun. Often the most trivial events will make people dissolve into laughter. Sometimes these are so small, in fact, that they cannot be recaptured in words. They are like the splash of the brook over a pebble, here one minute, gone the next, yet they are an attractive part of the flow of the stream. We have our laughs as a family, but most of the laughs are about such tiny things that the outsider might not appreciate them. So, if you have not a very developed sense of humour, this chapter may not appeal to you. Turn on to the deeper water-courses, but do not deny us the sparkling splash of family fun; it is a God-given relief sometimes.

We all loved the absent-minded member of the Committee who was constantly saying, "Oh dear, has anyone seen my glasses?" In the end, the family clubbed together to buy her a chain to put on her glasses so that she could wear them around her neck when not in use.

One day visitors arrived just as this lady was coming in from her car. Always ready to help, she went to meet them and assisted in escorting them round the house. Later that evening her husband was waiting patiently by the car to take his wife home. But she was frantically searching all the cloakrooms and bedrooms looking for her coat. It was finally discovered on the hedge in the garden where she had flung it in order that she might welcome the visitors who had arrived at the same time.

I evidently have a habit, borne of wishful thinking, I

suppose, when dictating letters to start: "This is just a short note . . .", whereupon I proceed to dictate a two-page letter! Since this came out in one of our famous skits, I must say I have tried to choose my words more appropriately.

One of the boys had such an urge to cook one day that he applied strong pressure on the girls in the kitchen. "All right", they said, "this week we shall be fewer than usual for meals—so go ahead with Thursday's lunch." There was an air of great mystery, many visits to the shops for this and that, and finally, half an hour late, he presented his masterpiece—spaghetti bolognaise. It was delicious, there was no denying it. The only snag was that he had made four times the amount required! Next day the boy went away to college, leaving the family to finish the food. Those dear people—they ploughed through that spaghetti bolognaise for dinner, tea and supper on Friday and Saturday until it was all eaten up! By Saturday evening they felt that they had spaghetti coming out of their ears! The lad had calculated that everyone would have as big an appetitite as his own.

When this boy first came to Torch House he had a certain amount of sight. However, he was touchy and could not be teased, especially if the teasing was remotely relevant to his poor sight. He would joke mercilessly at others' expense, but couldn't take it himself. Inside he was saying: "I'm going blind; don't you dare refer to it or make fun of it." He was on the defensive all the time, even in his fun. We watched the loving Hand of the Lord at work on him until that big "blind chip" rolled off his shoulder and he was able to laugh uproariously even about his mishaps due to blindness. He was now actually making fun of himself.

Our family have many experiences when out walking which often cause a laugh. One day, one of the boys went into Hurstpierpoint village, with his white cane held out in front of him—perhaps not quite in the correct manner. Suddenly he caught his stick smartly upon an obstacle. The "obstacle" straightened up, "What do you think you are doing, you blundering idiot, hitting me like that?" the obstacle snorted. The boy ascertained that the "obstacle" was an elderly man,

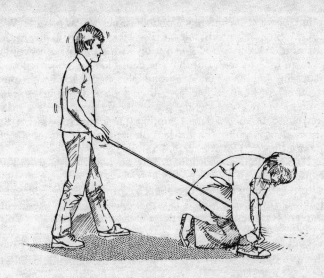

of medium height, and that he had been engaged in tying up his shoe-laces when the impact had occurred. "I'm sorry . . ." he began. "So you ought to be, barging along like that. You want to look where you're going!" "Sorry . . . but . . ." the boy couldn't get a word in. The old man followed him to the butcher's shop. "Keep your eyes open, you stupid thing, look where you're going!" The blind lad never did manage to tell the man that he couldn't see, however widely he opened his eyes. But he laughed! A big hurdle is overcome when we can see the funny side of such a situation.

Funny things happen at work too. One day one of the blind girls was marking up tapes in the recording department by sticking white labels on the cassettes. When the labels were fixed she used to go to the nearest sighted person, biro in hand, and ask them to write the titles on the labels. One day, peals of laughter greeted her request. Without knowing it, she had stuck Green Shield stamps on the tapes instead of labels!

Spontaneous laughter at funny stories and happenings is the one thing which we find most difficult to get across to the deaf-blind, because the manual alphabet is such a slow process. We found this quite difficult at Keswick in the Convention meetings. A very good illustration with a funny point would take so long to spell out that the deaf-blind person would be laughing loudly when everyone else had become serious again! Deaf-blind people have often got a very strong sense of humour. However, spelling out a joke on their hands is slow and cumbersome, and it is tempting at times not to pass it on to them. This is a pity, for the deaf-blind person needs the lift of humour more than any of us, I am sure.

P's shopping expedition to buy an outfit for a wedding caused a laugh. She inspected rows and rows of coats, carefully feeling the texture of each garment. Eventually, she found a fur coat. "Mm, I like this one—it's furry" she said loudly. Between giggles, her companion whispered, "You can't have that—it is already on someone!"

Shopping trips often have a funny side. One day, a very dreamy sighted helper offered to take an independent blind person to the shops. "I want to get some toothpaste" said the blind girl. "Do you want me to get it for you?" said her helper. "Oh no—I can manage!" She did. Next morning, she squeezed some on to her toothbrush, only to discover that she had bought a tube of shaving cream by mistake.

After a muddy walk one Sunday afternoon, Rona offered to go and collect Carol's shoes from the bedroom. "They are under the chair" said Carol. A puzzled Rona re-appeared downstairs a few minutes later carrying one black shoe and one brown—otherwise they were both identical. "Carol" she asked, "are these the shoes you want?" "That's right" said Carol. "But you can't wear them, they're not a pair. One is black and the other brown." Carol laughed. "Oh dear" she said. "So I have been wearing odd shoes all morning!"

A sighted visitor was surprised one day to see a figure emerge confidently from the bathroom where she had been washing her hair. Her face was completely swathed in a towel. The visitor watched the figure striding out towards the bedrooms, her eyes completely covered! It was then that she realised that it made no difference at all to a blind person whether the eyes were covered or not.

Yes, every family has its fun. The closer the family, the lovelier the fun. Perhaps the secret of successful teasing and joking is that fun must be linked closely with loving fellowship to really succeed.

One day, a blind fellow who was visiting us begged to be allowed to ride a bicycle. A sighted helper, always keen for adventure, offered to ride along the track in front of him ringing a bell. All went well for a few minutes, then the wind must have played a game, for the boy turned slightly and rode into a bank of stinging nettles! Undeterred, he picked himself up and rode all the way back home. Since then we have been given a tandem, which is much safer!

The store of fun grows with the years. Some of the family seem to be specially prone to "put their foot in it". Two girls went shopping one day in a discount store. One was quite blind, one was partially sighted. The blind girl wanted to buy four pairs of ladies pants. They chose the appropriate garments and reached the check-out. In a very loud voice the girl with a little sight said: "You are sure they will fit you now, aren't you!" "Yes" replied the other. The assistant coughed. "Hmm—we will change them if they are not suitable, madam" she said. Next day, the blind girl went off for a holiday. It was not until she had arrived that she discovered her mistake, for those pants were men's!

Humour reaches us from the regions too. Mrs. Harris had been a regular member of her Fellowship Group. She loved the Lord, and was very proud of her age, which she said was 95. She lived in the local Old People's Home, and was a bright witness there.

One day, the Registrar of the Fellowship Group noticed an obituary in the local paper. It was Mrs. Harris all right—and from the local Old People's Home. Poor dear, but still, 95 years is a good long time! The Registrar told the Chairman, and then the Committee. They decided that as she was such a lovely Christian, they must send a wreath and be at the funeral, as a witness to any unsaved relatives.

It was a very disappointing funeral service, just the bare

committal in a crematorium.

"Mrs. Harris would have wanted the Lord to be mentioned" said the Registrar to the Chairman. "Yes," he replied, "it was a bit chilling!" The Registrar went over to the bereaved son and told him that she knew his mother through the local Torch Group and what a marvellous old lady she was for 95.

"Yes" he replied. "Mother loved to come out to her clubs. But she was 84, not 95."

Oh well, old people do get muddled. The Registrar left it, went home and crossed Mrs. Harris off the register.

Next month the Fellowship Group started with chorus singing, and the Registrar was welcoming the folk as usual, when suddenly, skipping through the door to the chorus tune, came Mrs. Harris, all 95 years of her!

The deceased *was* Mrs. Harris, aged 84, who was not blind, and did not come to the Torch Fellowship!

"And we sent a wreath" said the somewhat chastened Registrar!

On another occasion, a lady was transporting people back from a Fellowship Group, when she inadvertently went through the traffic lights at red. She was stopped by a policeman: "Where have you come from?" he asked. "From the meeting of the Torch Trust for the Blind" she replied. He looked hard at her: "It looks like it!" he retorted.

Some incidents do not seem to be funny at the time, yet in retrospect they are hilarious.

One year, at the Family Houseparty, we had a number of families with babies and young children. Sue Oldham felt very sorry for one particular couple who seldom had an opportunity to go out together normally.

I'll baby-sit for you if you would like to go out to the service tonight" she said. The couple were very grateful and accepted the offer.

When the time came for people to leave for Church, Sue stood in the entrance lounge with the two babies she had promised to look after. Somehow word had gone round that Sue was running a baby-sitting service, and one by one, little ones were deposited with her, complete with bottles and detailed instructions to be followed.

Poor Sue! She was in quite a quandary. She didn't know which baby was which, and as for sorting out who had this milk and who had that, she had no idea!

At the time it was a nightmare, but eventually the babies were all fed and tucked into cots. Only two had been given the wrong feeds, and they all slept soundly until they could be sorted out by their rightful parents.

"We'll organise a crèche properly another time" said Sue firmly.

There is a time to laugh. So many of the folk who find their way to us have had no time to laugh at all throughout their childhood and youth. We are glad to see them laughing now.

CHAPTER EIGHT — FIERY TRIAL

We had arrived! Hallaton was gradually taking shape, and although a lot still remained to be done to the house, it was exciting to see how much we *had* done.

The work in the Fellowship Groups was going ahead with very little need for extra stimulus, the literature work was growing, with plenty of room for expansion in large print. The tape department was not yet fully operative, for we still needed a technician but, all told, the work was progressing well.

Then, into the ranks crept the same complaint which attacked the Hebrews on their epic journey to Canaan—criticism! Now, no work of men exists which is above having anything wrong with it, and a loving, constructive critic is invaluable—as Moses found when Jethro suggested improvements in his judicial system. But criticism behind people's backs, fault-finding with no knowledge of the facts, or worse, relying on faulty information—this is evil. It promotes other evils too, the pride which says "Now *I* would be able to do this better", the bitterness which imagines slights and insults, and the general grumbling which spreads like cancer. Criticism which causes these things is well described in Galatians 5:19 ". . . hatred, quarrelling, jealousy, bad temper, rivalry, factions, party spirit, envy . . . and things like that." How opposite these things are to the work of the Spirit of God in producing fruit in our lives.

The main body of our staff did not want to be party to this

disease of criticism, but it is hard to be subjected to it, like a constant drip, drip, and not to be affected. The criticism was levelled at our Communion at first, and our Bible study, and eventually at the whole leadership. Strange to say our Communion and Bible study were the two events in our week which had been singled out by visitors as of great spiritual blessing to them. Some folk even came from other parts to join us on those occasions, and we were blessed. However, even the most blessed things if they are regularly given to us, tend to be taken for granted. Just a few of the staff were not able to understand the Bible study, because they needed simpler teaching. Ultimately, we arranged a special time for them. But one or two others, because of the criticisms levelled at us from outside, began to want more "life" or freedom and the exercise of charismatic gifts on a larger scale. Up to this time we had been conscious of a growing warmth and freedom in our worship, which had rejoiced our hearts! We could see people who had been inhibited before who were losing their inhibitions, as they poured their hearts out in praise to God. However, the critics were in a hurry, and pressed beyond what we felt was the Holy Spirit's leading. It was sad to see how Satan drove and tore the flock of God entrusted to us at this time. It was sad, too, to see evidence of sin and wrong ambition in the forces gathered against us. Then the leadership was challenged, and an effort was made to get rid of the "Torch Family" image with Mum and Dad and brothers and sisters, and to substitute a structured community with very rigid rules, and over-emphasized subjection under church order.

It was a time of deep trial and pain to us all. We looked around at the unloved people who had found shelter with us, folk whom we knew God had sent to us. He had "Set the solitary in families" indeed. We knew that their lives, up to joining us, had been in some cases, cruelly restricted by too much discipline, without love. True, there was need to encourage them to do a useful job of work where they could, and where such a job existed, but in other ways their behaviour was orderly and well-disciplined because they were beginning to be loved and to love, and to *want* to be helpful.

As the family had grown around us, we had spent many hours before the Lord, asking Him to give us His direction. We felt sure we had His blessing on the present family system. We felt sure that He was giving us the fellowship of several "leaders", people who were willing to take a larger share of responsibility in the family, thus spreading the load. Some of these leaders have stood with us throughout the fiery trial with unswerving love and loyalty, just as David's three mighty men did when all the others fled. We deeply appreciate these warriors, and praise God for them. They did not say "yes" to every suggestion, oh no! But they had knowledge and love behind every counter-suggestion which we were glad to acknowledge.

Personally, we fought a deep battle. Had the time come for us to retire? We had nowhere to go, of course, for all we had was tied up with the work, but God could easily solve that problem if it was His will. And who would take over? The critics had proved by their behaviour and attitudes that they were not suitable, and though the leaders were coming on well, they were not ready yet for full leadership.

"Lord, it would simplify things if You just let us die" we said, for our sore hearts were grieved to breaking-point. We loved those who were raising their voices against us, they were our friends. It made it all the harder.

Then the Lord began to show us, in a multitude of little ways, that we *were* in the place He had appointed for us, that this was but an all-out attack of the enemy to stop a work which was hurting him too much, and that it was aimed especially at us because, in our counselling, there were times when we found ourselves fighting the very powers of darkness themselves. By this time we could rejoice in several "hopeless" people who had been released from the enemy's clutches. No wonder he hated us so badly!

This was a time of great self-examination, a testing of motives and methods, and daily laying the whole work before the Lord for Him to correct and adjust as He wanted. But it was also a time when we were lashed by rumours and reports which were distorted.

It was July 1977, and time for us to go to Keswick with the houseparty. Keswick—the place where people through the years have been able to open their hearts before the all-seeing eye of God. And that was what we wanted. As far as *we* could judge we *had* obeyed Him, and sought to be clean and pure in His sight. But maybe we had something hidden which was grieving Him, maybe our critics had a grain of truth in their condemnation—maybe . . . ! "Search me, O God . . . . ; try me, ... and see if there be any wicked way in me" became our constant prayer.

We prayed earnestly for a word from the Lord, even if it was one of rebuke.

I well remember going into that first meeting in the tent at Keswick, almost expecting a painful heart-searching. But the message, which centred on the glory of the Lord, was one of warm encouragement especially to "broken-hearted leaders" who had been harassed and attacked by criticism and pressure. We felt our hearts melt before God. He knew, and He cared! All through that week, this note was struck until I felt that Keswick 1977 must have been planned with us in mind!

Inspite of such encouragements, there were times when we wondered if we should "give up". I voiced this thought to one friend who pointed out that Miss Trench, who first thought of Torch, was eighty-three when she retired. She waited until she was sure that it was the right time for her to hand over to us. It would not be because of pressure and difficulty that we should retire, but in the wise leading of God, who would have the successors ready to continue His work.

But we did long to be away from the fiery trial! We could understand Paul, who had the desire to depart and be with Christ which is far better.

The last time we doubted and were reassured, was at a houseparty to which we went privately for fellowship. The day we were going, I felt especially low. "Oh Lord, how long? Why can't I just lie down and die?" Just as if I had heard a voice, came the words, "Go into your lounge and read a poem in a book by Amy Carmichael." I was rather puzzled because I was not in the habit of reading poetry. However, I obeyed. I read:

> "O Lord, when I'm weary with toiling,
> And burdensome seem Thy commands;
> If my load should lead to complaining,
> Lord, show me Thy hands.
> Thy nail-pierced hands, Thy cross-torn hands!
> My Saviour, show me Thy hands.
>
> O Christ, if ever my footsteps should falter,
> And I be prepared for retreat;
> If desert and thorn cause lamenting,
> Lord, show me Thy feet.
> Thy bleeding feet, Thy nail-scarred feet!
> Lord Jesus, show me Thy feet.
>
> O Lord, when I am sorely wounded
> With the battle and toil of the day;
> And I complain of my suffering,
> Lord, let me hear Thee say—
> 'Behold My side, My spear-pierced side,
> My side that was wounded for thee.'

My God! Dare I show Thee *my* hands and *my* feet?"

Selected.
Author not known

"O Christ, if ever my footsteps should falter, and I be prepared for retreat"! I bowed my head and prayed, "Lord, truly I have been tempted to retreat, but when I look at Your feet and then at mine, I am ashamed. Help me to follow, and not to talk of retreat."

We went to the houseparty, and enjoyed fellowship and love there. The first talk was dealing with the peace of God in service. It was given in the form of a testimony by that dear retired evangelist, Marshall Shallis. Each word ministered comfort to our hearts. Then as he finished his talk, he pulled out a piece of paper. "I want to close with a poem" he said, and he read the very same poem which I had been reading so recently. We went up to our room, with a sense of holy awe and wonder. We accepted the fact that God Himself had spoken to us. He had forbidden the retreat which our flesh longed for.

A few days later I thought I would look at the poem again. Search as I would, I couldn't find it! No matter, its message had been used by the Holy Spirit to brace us, and recommission us to the task committed to our care.

The whole of the period was one of heartache, and it was very puzzling too for others, including the staff, who were not aware of all sides of the problem. We felt unable to share, in fact we felt the Lord had specifically told us to "stand still and see the salvation of the Lord". To share all meant to disclose another's very serious shortcomings and who were we to do that?

Throughout this time the Committee was a great source of inspiration, and correction too. We were truly blessed by their help and love.

As we look back, we are glad that never once did we make a move to sever fellowship, but were able to extend hands of love even though they were ignored.

But fiery trials are not sent for fun. They have a purpose which is eternal, a "far more exceeding weight of glory". Some of this glory we can see already, some is in formation still; the final tally, the purest gold, will be seen in eternity itself.

Gradually, the storm passed. Apart from one or two small spots, there was light and understanding throughout our big family. "Be not overcome of evil, but overcome evil with good" became a very real challenge when faced with a few who did not know the truth.

And the main body of staff were left more united, and more determined not to "murmur", more dedicated than ever before to the task they had set themselves to. We had to say "Goodbye" to the few who were the chief murmurers. They were our loved colleagues and we felt their going keenly. Yet, right through the family, there was a sense of relief when they had gone. If only they had known . . . But we knew that we must leave the Lord to show them. And maybe He did plan for them to move on. A certain amount of moving can be helpful in any work. New scenes of labour can provide the right opportunities to use lessons learned in other places. Often new staff coming to us have been amazed at how their past has been a preparation for their present work. It is, however, a very sad experience when movement of staff is accompanied by bitterness and recrimination. This does not glorify God, although He wonderfully controls it and turns it to good.

We were beginning to see the good, the gold from the trials, and, as one visitor said at this time—"Coming here this time has been like seeing little shoots of green growth breaking out everywhere".

Little shoots of green growth! The Lord began to touch us in a new way. People received spiritual, mental and physical healing. And when we went out to testify to the goodness of the Lord, folk began asking for help, for counsel and prayer. Some found the Lord Jesus Christ as their Saviour. We were well aware that this was nothing to do with our ability—it was the Lord's work. We were glad to have had to endure the chastening.

But then, just as we thought the trials were over, another attack came. We tasted the pain of being betrayed by one we held dear, the trial of being scourged with "the strife of tongues". Once again words which we had said were wrongly reported, truth was twisted grotesquely, until some of our acquaintances looked at us with questioning eyes, and cold barriers rose between us, which we longed to see broken down. It was tempting to shout the truth loud and clear, and to expose the lies of the enemy but, whilst the truth must be spoken, it must not be in any spirit of self-vindication. The Word of God to us in this further trial was "He will bring forth your vindication as the light, and your right as the noon day". (Psalm 37:6) He, the Lord God Himself, would do it! And indeed He did!

We are living in evil times. Our Lord warned us that evil would wax worse and worse. And "All that will live godly in Christ Jesus shall suffer persecution". (II Timothy 3:12) So we should not be taken by surprise when suffering comes our way. However, we praise God that in all things He does have the victory, and through these very trials He leads us into a closer walk with Himself, and into a deeper realisation of His worthiness and His power.

CHAPTER 9 — HOUSEPARTIES

When we think back to the early days and to the houseparties which we held then, we can see that like everything else in the Torch Family, houseparties have "developed". There has been an imperceptible difference which is hard to actually put into words. Perhaps it has been a mellowing, a deepening of the work, a greater expectation when we have prayed for blessing. Yet, we are aware that we still have a lot to learn, for we are discovering how much we need to be open to the working of the Holy Spirit to know when and how much to plan, and when to leave free time for whatever we might be led into.

It has become necessary for us to specialise a little when arranging houseparties. Regional representatives, library workers, families, young people, the deaf-blind and social workers all have a claim upon our thoughts as we plan our programme. This makes it more necessary to have a few houseparties which are open to any who do not fit into a set category. As one thirty-year-old girl put it: "I'm not eligible for any of your special houseparties now; I feel a reject!" Easter time is one of the open houseparties, when we have a special emphasis on missionary interest, and try to have missionaries on furlough to talk to us. Then we have holiday weeks in the summer which are arranged with more leisure time than weekend houseparties. They include a morning devotional and a very relaxed programme for the evenings, with some organised outings in the afternoons. Smaller houseparties are held too at "Little Torch", where we often have difficulty in accommodating all the people who want to go. At the specialised houseparties, specific problems are prayed over, discussed and suggestions are made for improvements. The Regional and Library Workers' weekends are rather intense, as there is such a lot to be packed into the programme. We have seen some of our poor visitors almost wilt as they have tried to soak up all the information which they have been given in such concentrated form!

However, most houseparties are convened for spiritual uplift and refreshment, and are taken in a more leisurely manner. Family Houseparty is a time when the boys and girls are given their own programme, with treasure hunts in the grounds, and quizzes laid on for them. Different members of staff take on responsibilities for the houseparties, so that the load does not fall on one or two.

The Committee help too. I seem to remember Ken Blackmore sitting on a wall, trying to look like Humpty Dumpty! At one Family Houseparty we had such a lot of unattached, single girls and fellows that we asked the families to extend and include some of these. This brought about some lovely friendships, as well as helping with the family competitions. When, after several tries, there were still a few spare people, they banded together and labelled themselves, "The Orphans". It was surprising how quickly they found a

71

Mum and Dad after that!

Young People's Houseparties are times of outreach and have been wonderfully blessed. Many of those who found faith in the Lord Jesus have come the next year to learn more, which has been most encouraging. One year, before we moved, accommodation was a real problem, and we had to hire tents and pitch them in a nearby field. The weather was hot and sunny, and the camp was a great success. The boys loved it!

Most ingenious games are played at houseparties for the young people. We had a patriarch's race once, when some of us older folk were put in armchairs and carried down the field by our "tribes". It was a miracle that bones were not broken that day, as the "tribes" became so excited, that they tipped the chairs over! There were other ingenious competitions, such as timing a team who had to fill a bucket from a distant tap using a hosepipe cut into six pieces. Some of the staff seem to have exceptionally inventive minds. The young folk love this, the extroverts participate, and the others stand and laugh! We even had a mobility race once, with sighted staff walking the course blind-fold!

It is amazing how many pieces of equipment go wrong during houseparties, from light bulbs to tea urns. And, it seems that the extra vibration of a hundred feet loosens every bit of plaster which is insecure! The maintenance staff have to keep constant watch for hanging ceilings, blocked drains and other minor problems.

The Holy Spirit moves in most unorthodox ways at houseparties, and we find people deeply touched when there has been no particular human agency used to convict them. At one houseparty, before the first lights out, a young fellow fell on his knees and asked the Lord to save him. At a Communion Service someone else came to Christ. Yet another boy was so anxious to find peace that he couldn't wait for the speaker to finish his bath, and called out his question through the bathroom door. It is a very humbling experience to see God at work, but we need to watch, lest we expect it to come automatically!

Although at Torch we do not frame our worship on any particular denominational pattern, we do arrange for the ordinance of believers' baptism if it is requested. One year, a very young girl asked us if she could be baptised during a houseparty. She had been at boarding school most of her life, and she was not even sure where "home" would be when she left school. She loved the Lord Jesus dearly, and did so want to be baptised. After a lot of prayer, we felt we should use the swimming pool and have a baptismal service in the garden. By the time the hour had come, eight other young people had come forward and asked to be baptised, each with no real opportunity of being baptised in their local surroundings, and each one a true believer. We rigged up an amplification system, and sat around the pool in very hot sunshine. It was a great thrill to hear those young people give their testimonies and say clearly: "Jesus Christ is Lord". People from the village came in and wondered. "We haven't seen anything like this before," they said! Both of the summer houseparties witnessed similar scenes that year. That was when Dad Heath earned the title, "Ron the Baptist"!

At the beginning of one houseparty, we were so deeply moved by the many needy people who had come together, that we hardly knew how to face them all. They were so hungry for spiritual food, so longing for the best that God could give them. It was good to see the way their needs were met, and in many cases we noticed their joyfulness as they went home satisfied. Sometimes, however, they had to go back to such difficult places that they almost broke down at the thought of leaving the warmth of love and fellowship.

Comparing notes on the houseparty afterwards is always a time for praise, though it also highlights the need to keep in touch with the folk after they have gone home. "I've promised to write to L every week", said one of our staff. L was a mentally retarded girl, unable to take in very much. The staff members kept up their contact with her faithfully. Then there was the girl who wept because she thought we would not allow her to be baptised. It appears that although she loved the Lord, she could not read, much as she tried. She was sure this would hinder her from following the Lord in baptism. It was amazing, and just like the Lord, that we were given a cassette machine and cassettes of Scripture recordings the very next week, which we were able to pass on to her.

One helper found two girls in earnest conversation in the bedroom. The sighted one was looking down the index at the front of a Bible. "There isn't anything like that, honest", she said, closing the book. "There is", said the blind girl, "It is S-A-R-M-S, I think".

"Well, I've looked all down the list and I can't find it." The helper had to smile, as she showed them where to find Psalms. "Oh well, how was I to know it began with a P".

She found the two girls later, looking at verse 23 in every Psalm, because someone had told them that Psalm 23 was lovely. They enjoyed it together later on, and came to know the Lord as their own Shepherd.

Reactions differ; one girl was thrilled with everything, but she didn't show it at all—in fact, we wondered if she was unhappy. She wrote a very full, glowing letter when she got home, telling us of her new-found faith. On the other hand, a boy, newly blinded, came to one houseparty and hated it. The fun, the laughter, the singing, all grated on him. "I want to go home", he shouted. "It's hell here!" We certainly never know what we shall meet at a houseparty.

We have only recounted doings at houseparties held at Torch House. More and more of the regions are holding their own local houseparties, and are having great times of renewal and blessing. We also have regular houseparties at the Keswick Convention. We have known the weather to be warm and sunny, we have known it to be terribly wet. Mostly, it is somewhere in between! The greatest joy of Keswick, apart from the Convention meetings, is the opportunity of fellowship together. We ourselves enjoy this, as we have no responsibility for catering, nor organising the ministry. This gives us time to get close to the folk in our party, to pray with them and share spiritual joys and experiences. Meeting with other Christians, visiting the stalls and thus having an insight into missionary work, are all part of the value of Keswick. These are rich times, enhanced too by the spiritual feasts which are given from the Keswick platform. We try to have outings in the afternoons of the Convention Week. We take some of the blind people for really good walks—something which many of them long for at home, but are not able to have.

Houseparties are certainly not everyone's idea of a holiday. Some of our staff quite dread them, and usually get on with their work in a quiet corner while the houseparties are in progress. It is part of the wonder of life that the Lord has made us all so different. The way He meets our needs, varied as they are, is evidence of His care for us as individuals. He understands the folk who prefer to be in smaller groups. However, we are impressed as we look back, to see how many people have found new life and eternal blessing at houseparties. They certainly suit some.

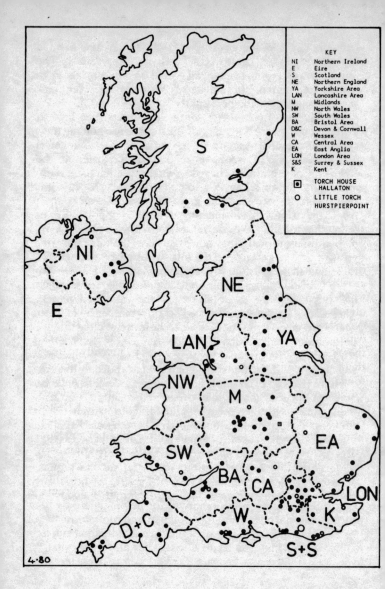

KEY

NI	Northern Ireland
E	Eire
S	Scotland
NE	Northern England
YA	Yorkshire Area
LAN	Lancashire Area
M	Midlands
NW	North Wales
SW	South Wales
BA	Bristol Area
D&C	Devon & Cornwall
W	Wessex
CA	Central Area
EA	East Anglia
LON	London Area
S&S	Surrey & Sussex
K	Kent

⊡ TORCH HOUSE
   HALLATON

○ LITTLE TORCH
   HURSTPIERPOINT

4·80

CHAPTER 10 — ROUND THE REGIONS

One of the areas where the growth of the Torch Family is most noticeable is in the regional side of the work. Since 1970 when, under the Hand of God Peter Jackson had the vision to start the first Fellowship Group in Birmingham, Groups have formed in most big towns and cities. However, the rate of the growth of Fellowship Groups reflects some valuable lessons which we have had to learn. At first we moved quickly, plunging straight into the work with anyone who would help. As a result, Fellowship Groups sprang up all over Britain within the first five years. Time has shown that in some cases these Groups formed before the committee were ready to take the responsibility. Nowadays we prefer to see a prayer foundation laid before moving forward into forming a new Group. Any new Fellowship Group needs to start as a Prayer Group. Prayer is a wonderful unifying power. We all have to come to the Lord on the same basis, through Jesus Christ our Lord and Saviour. So, if a group of people, blind or sighted, feel led to form a Torch Fellowship Group in their locality, we say: "Get praying!"

Some folk have been known to discover that they are not truly the Lord's children as they try to take part in a Prayer Group. Sometimes people's motives for helping are only to provide material comfort to the visually handicapped. As the Prayer Group begins to function, they see that the real aim is to love and win blind people to Christ. They may, as they talk over these differences, find that the very centre of their own life is empty and purposeless. Occasionally, the motive for helping with a Group may be: "I want to get these people to my church", rather than to show them love in Christ. Praying together brings a one-ness which supercedes denominational barriers and shows up those who are in bondage to any particular form of worship. Sometimes members of the Prayer Groups encounter difficulties with each other's personalities, and need to pray for grace, love and understanding. It is much better to discover these things before a Fellowship Group is started! Usually, members of the Group grow to love each other deeply, and have wonderful fellowship together. When this is the case, it augurs well for the future of the Fellowship, and also for the work of Torch in that region.

The difficulties which have arisen in Fellowship Groups have usually appeared in those which started without the basis of a Prayer Group. The emphasis on prayer is something which is woven into all aspects of the work of Torch. The central Committee, which shoulders the over-all responsibility, always starts with at least half-an-hour of prayer, with everyone participating. How can we deliberate, decide and direct others if we have not bowed the knee to the Highest Authority?

As in all Torch Committees, (or prayer and planning groups, as some prefer to call them), we do not vote. We are sure that in work for God, we are not intended to be a democracy—government by the people—with its voting and minorities, and the assumption that the majority is always right. We believe firmly in Theocracy, government by the All-Wise, All-Knowing, All-Powerful God, available to us through the atoning work of Jesus Christ, and revealed to us by the infilling of the Holy Spirit. Some might shake their heads and say: "Visionary—that's all right on paper, but I can't see it working". Well, why not? Is the Holy Spirit unable to bring unity and to direct all of the Committee? We believe He *is* able. If we differ, we realise that we must leave discussing the matter and get before God about it. We don't want good ideas from man, but the power and direction of the Holy Spirit. He is able to speak to all of us, and so we must leave any decision about which there is a question, so that it can be resolved by prayer. We may sound far too naive—we probably are—but where the love of Christ prevails, we are proving that this method works.

As the Prayer Group develops, the abilities of each member begin to be recognised. Soon a leader emerges, a secretary, a treasurer, a registrar and others to do the catering, visiting and organising of transport. When the Group prays together about the needs of local blind people, it is surprising how many visually handicapped are brought to its notice. In the end the members feel they should wait no longer, and they send in a note to Torch House: "We want to inaugurate on such and such a date. Can you send someone to be at our first meeting?" The gestation period is over; another Fellowship Group has come to the birth!

The surprises begin. "I didn't know *any* visually handicapped people before—I'm surprised to see so many here!" One member of a Prayer Group saw a slight accident; a blind lady tripped over a chain which was hanging between two posts. She ran to help her, and discovered that she lived near to her. Next week a Fellowship Group was inaugurating, so she took the blind lady along. Other workers discovered blind neighbours who hadn't spoken to each other for a long time over some very small disagreement—they were willing to come, but not to travel in the same car, and not to sit near each other! A clear need here for the Gospel message! Many folk who come to a Fellowship Group have no means of reading Christian literature. A number might have "talking books"—praise God we have cassettes for them; some might read braille, or moon type, but the majority very often have nothing but their radios. Some of them listen to anything with complete credulity, and when they do talk about spiritual things, the hotch-potch of beliefs which tumble out can be very negative, misleading and grossly untrue, when measured by the standard of Holy Scripture. Such people often come to the Fellowship Group with a real hunger to know the truth, and a dissatisfaction with their "religious" experiences. Two things very much welcomed by new contacts at a Fellowship

Group are the small cassettes which can be played back on commercial cassette machines, and the Torch-size large print. Once people have the opportunity to hear what God says, their beliefs become more clearly defined. Then they have a completely new outlook, because they are able to come face to face with Christ.

"It is much too hard to try to preach to old people—they are so set in their ways", said one worker to us. Sometimes the minds of the elderly are unable to grasp anything new, but we know of an amazing number in their eighties who are rejuvenated by the experience of new birth. One elderly sighted husband was so surprised to see the love which was shown to his blind wife at a Fellowship Group, that he went to church to learn more about it. He came to Christ. "My life has begun all over again at eighty-four!" he exclaimed. And there are others. The Holy Spirit can penetrate the minds of the elderly and give them new life. Some Fellowships in retirement areas find that most of their blind folk are elderly. Loneliness is a big problem to them. "I have not had anyone in to read my letters for a month" someone said. Visitors from a Fellowship Group can help a great deal. Ill-health, bereavement, coping with the shopping and mobility are problems met with when the majority of the folk are elderly.

In industrial towns, however, there are more working blind people. This reflects on the type of programme required at the Fellowship meetings, but the need to hear the Gospel and to have Christian literature in some form is the same. Other problems are met with, which are common to all—marital difficulties, work situations, the need for help with personal shopping, heartaches over children—in fact, all the range of human need.

In some areas there is need for a separate meeting for young people, maybe in the evening, usually informally in a home. Here young folk can be encouraged to discuss spiritual things, to study and to read, and of course, to enjoy Christian music.

Problems arise when one or two young folk turn up in an area which is predominantly elderly. If there are enough young ones, and sighted young people are available, then it usually works well. One Fellowship encourages their young folk to form a group to sing at the meetings and also in local churches; another makes sure that at least some of the programme will interest the young. Sometimes blind young folk like to help. It is surprising how many ways there are of ensuring a welcome to all ages.

It would be very one-sided if we didn't mention the blessing experienced by sighted people. All Torch activities aim to be totally integrated—ideally, half the number blind and half sighted. This makes for an enlarged circle of friends and interests, and helps a great deal with practical things like handing out tea, or walking when on an outing. Where do the sighted people come from? A nucleus come from local churches and they are often contacted through deputation meetings. Others come in because they hear about the Fellowship Group from friends, and want to help. Some have come to help and have found Christ! Many have been blessed by contact with radiant Christians who have triumphed over a visual handicap. Young people from church youth groups and schools have all played their part too.

Just a few areas have special needs, where there are centres for the doubly handicapped, for example, and where there is a concentration of deaf-blind people. The manual alphabet is not difficult to learn, and a conversation "spelled out" can bring great joy to a deaf-blind person. We are glad that a number of Fellowship Groups are getting to grips with this need.

As we visit Fellowship Groups we are most interested to see the variety of methods used and the "local flavour" which comes over. It is even more varied than the attractive birthday cakes which a lot of Groups produce on the celebration of their inaugural meeting. Some people have splendid teas, a few have just biscuits; one has tea in the middle of the time together, and this lengthens the whole proceeding to three hours! Quizzes go down well in some areas too.

One Fellowship found itself with a high proportion of slightly mentally-retarded people. An orthodox meeting every time did not meet the need. Then they remembered the old Sunday School idea of splitting into small groups. They opened their time together by singing simple choruses, they had a Bible reading, then divided for discussion on the reading. In these small groups some of the folk blossomed! Several of them were able to share for the first time how they came to know and love the Lord. Yes, methods can vary—but the message is the same.

Looking back we have many memories of visits to Fellowship Groups, and to clubs, hostels and workshops, and to blind people in their own homes. Reviewing these is like looking at a kaleidoscope with patterns bright and dark, humorous and sad, yet when the light of Jesus shines in on the patterns, they become beautiful. Here are a few pieces from the kaleidoscope!

An elderly blind couple at an inaugural meeting sat and wept. "What is the matter? Haven't you enjoyed it?" asked an anxious worker. "It isn't that —we've been waiting for something like this to happen. We wanted to hear this a long time ago." The Light did shine on that couple!

"Would you like to have a Talking Book?" asked a worker.

"Yes, I think I will, but I'm not religious", was the reply. "What about having a missionary story?" "Oh no, not a missionary story." The worker tried again. 'Well, would you like a biography of a missionary?" "Oh, yes, I'd like that. Yes, that would be all right." That lady is still in the "dark", but she has access to material which can bring her into the Light of Christ.

"I'm not religious, you know. I hardly ever went to Church before I became blind, so I certainly wouldn't go now. That would be hypocrisy, wouldn't it?" said one. Yet this lady goes faithfully to a Fellowship Group; another one waiting for the Light.

"You will come for me next time: you won't forget will you? I've had so many disappointments that I find it easier never to expect anything good, and then I'm not hurt", exclaimed one lady. What a friend she can have in Jesus, Who never lets us down. What a responsibility rests on the workers to keep faithfully to what they promise to do.

Fellowship Groups soon find they have to take on other activities. Recordings of books are sometimes supplied from the Tape Library in quantity to Fellowships, so that they can operate a sub-library. In this way the readers can talk about the books they have just brought back, or recommend them to their friends, or have a chance to ask any questions. But some Fellowship Groups have taken on the task of making recordings of their own, with a simple message and plenty of singing. This is an area of the work which is very useful when visiting those who are too ill or too infirm to come to the Fellowship Group itself.

Another development in some areas has been Regional Houseparties. A suitable conference centre not too far away is taken as a meeting-place for people from a number of Groups in an area. On these occasions folk very often get their first taste of a Christian home environment. They have a break right away from normal pressures, have opportunities to sing, to hear about the Lord, to talk to new people, and to begin to see the relevance of the Christian message to their daily lives.

Regional Conference used to take place once a year at

Hallaton, but we very quickly outgrew the premises there for one single gathering, and so we have a series of two or three weekends for representatives from the regions. This has several disadvantages, not the least being that we have to go through the same programme two or three times. However, delegates appreciate being able to visit the Family Home, and to see the studios and production units. We arrange alternating dates for each region so that North, South, East and West can meet each other over the years.

Members of the central Committee try to visit the workers in the Fellowship Groups when they happen to be in their area. These times are valuable, as we are able to share our problems, and discuss ways of satisfying the needs still to be met. Often we can pass on the solution which one Group has found to another Group with the same problem. Literature requirements can be discovered too, which help us in future planning.

At times, members from the Committees in an area join together to plan other activities such as rallies, which give opportunity for folk from different Fellowship Groups to meet each other. These can be very helpful and foster the links which are very much part of Fellowship Group work.

Fellowship and love are two attributes in short supply these days. Yet when Christians sink their differences, and get together to work for others, then these two beautiful qualities blossom. And, when you think about it, didn't the Lord Himself promise a special blessing to those who stretched out their hands to the blind? "When thou makest a feast, call the poor, the lame, the blind, and thou shalt be blessed."(Luke 14:13–14) Many workers in Fellowship Groups would testify to the fact that this is very true in their lives.

CHAPTER 11 — BRISTOL FASHION

"Mum, can we stage a play in the garage?" The three Hyde children were full of ideas like this.

"Yes", their mother replied, glad to see them, happily occupied.

Later on they came to her with £3.50, the takings from their play, and asked for it to go to the blind.

Rachel Hyde pondered the matter. Where could she send it? As a Christian she felt she would like to see it put into Christian Work. Then she came across the little testimony booklet, "Treasures of Darkness", and noticed the information at the back of the book about the work of the Torch Trust. This was the beginning of a real interest in the work of Torch. It was further stimulated by the fact that the Hyde family lived in the same road as Wendy, the first blind girl we ever met. Wendy and Dudley and their little boy, Joseph, were so glad to have the fellowship and practical help which Rachel and her family readily gave.

When we began to think about forming a Torch Fellowship Group in Bristol, we sent invitations to all our prayer partners so that they could meet us and discuss plans. This was before the days when we established Prayer Groups first. Just a few people, including Rachel, responded to the invitation, and a Group was started.

The new Group was small and struggling for quite a time. Most of the Committee were ladies, and as they visited blind folk in the area, they were amazed at the extent of the need. They decided that they must let other Christians know, in the hope that helpers would come forward to take over some of the work. The result was not too encouraging. However, they did not give up. One day an invitation came to them asking them to talk about the work of Torch at an Assembly of Christian Brethren. "We will gladly come," they said, "but we are only women. I'm afraid we have no men now to help us." "That will be all right", the brother replied.

On the actual day when they arrived at the Hall, that particular brother was not there. "We're from the Torch Trust for the Blind", the ladies said. "Oh yes," said the elder at the door, "but where is your speaker?" Feeling very embarrassed, the ladies said, "We are the speakers. You see we have no men. We're very sorry!" The brethren were very kind, and the ladies were given the opportunity to put the local needs before the Assembly. The very fact that they had no men to speak for them added urgency to their message. Two men volunteered from that meeting, and have been a great tower of strength to the work in Bristol ever since.

After this there was a break-through in Bristol, and the work surged forward. The Fellowship Group grew so large that it was decided to divide it into two, North-East and North-West. At the first meeting of the new Group, ten people went from the original Group to the new one to encourage it, and a team of four went from Torch House. They found eighty-four people at the first meeting! It was obvious that other Groups were needed. In fact, a short while later, another one was started at Bristol South.

All this time God was at work preparing yet more help for the blind and partially-sighted people of Bristol. Liz Gould had come to that very first meeting held to form a Fellowship Group. She had a blind girl staying with her, so she thought it might be an idea to take her along. Liz became interested in helping the newly-formed Committee which was trying to organise a Torch Fellowship Group, and offered to find a hall for the meeting. Liz had previous links with blind people, so her help was eagerly sought to find blind folk in the neighbourhood and to encourage them to come to the Fellowship.

But God was working in Liz, calling her to a commitment to the task of running a Fellowship Group. Should she get involved whole-heartedly in the Bristol Group? Liz wasn't strong, and she was already fully committed to the work in her Church. She took her thoughts to the Lord in prayer, and the Lord showed her through the text, "The joy of the Lord is your strength", that it was His will that she should take up the work. Soon she became secretary of that first Bristol Group.

But it was obvious that there was a need for a full-time visitor to make an impact on the lonely, isolated blind people in the Bristol area. Liz felt her heart moved with longing to help on a full-time basis. It was at this time that the Church which Liz attended, seeing the obvious call of God that Liz had heard, separated her to the work of the Gospel among the blind, and released her from some of her duties in the Church.

We had many a discussion and much prayer with the Bristol Committee about the possibility of Liz being our first full-time field-worker. We all realised that this was a big venture, and might well be the forerunner of developments in other areas. We wanted to be sure that we knew what was God's will. The question of training had to be faced, and it seemed right that Liz should spend time at Headquarters to have an opportunity to become part of the Family. So Liz gave in her notice from teaching, and came up to Torch House for a period.

As Liz had previously worked in the Bristol Blind School, which was later closed, she had some experience of work amongst young blind folk. At Hallaton she met all sorts, teenagers and early twenties who had been subjected to much that had spoiled their lives, visitors who came hungry for fellowship and, through the Tape Library, she came in contact with the needy elderly blind, as she selected books for them to hear.

Liz reckons that the Lord had more than one object in mind when He kept her at Torch House for three years. She feels strongly that any full-time Regional Worker should have a long period at Headquarters. "You can cover your weaknesses for a short while," she said, "but the reality is shown over a period. And it is good to see how during this time fellowship can grow deeper!"

During her period at Torch House, Liz kept in faithful and constant touch with the Bristol scene, sharing joys, problems, sorrows and keeping a strong link between them and us at Headquarters. It was a valuable period for us all.

At last, the Lord moved Liz out. A flat was found which was ideal, in the house of a Fellowship Group worker. It had already been let, but the letting fell through just at the time Liz was making enquiries.

Liz had already been provided with a car and, as she started her visitation programme, she realised how essential it was to have transport. The car was very useful for shopping trips and for taking people to hospital and, of course, there was always braille, moon, large print and cassettes to be taken with her as she went the rounds.

Now Liz is liaising with all the Groups in the Bristol area. When she hears of a blind person in need, sometimes referred to her by Welfare, she can link them to the Fellowship Group nearest to them. Similarly, the Fellowship Group Committees provide her with a list of those who they feel would benefit from having a visit.

It might be helpful for us to look at Liz as she starts out for a typical day's work.

The first visit is to a block of flats—how lonely these places can be! The first person on the list is not at home, so Liz leaves a note, hoping the lady will find someone who can read it to her. The lady next on the visiting list has bought some curtains, and is glad when Liz offers to hang them for her. Liz has recently spent a day helping an arthritic lady to move house, so she is getting used to handling curtains.

It is twelve storeys up for the next visit, to an elderly lady who spends hours looking wistfully out of the window, with the little sight she has left. "It is so lonely here sometimes," she says. "I get a bit depressed with it." Liz has a little Bible reading and prayer with her before leaving.

An old people's Home is the next call. The blind lady here is very crippled, and has so little to live for! She loves to have cassettes from Marjorie Mason, and tapes of the Torch choir.

Another visit provides a lady with more large print books, and another blind lady is encouraged to read Christian braille books from the Torch library. Liz arranges to take some of the people she visits for a holiday to Torch House in the summer.

A deaf-blind man is visited too. As he can't read by touch at all, Liz arranges for him to have a weekly visit so that the Scriptures can be spelt on his hand. It took a year to read through St. Luke's Gospel in this way.

Not one of the people Liz visits has ever refused when she asks if she can pray before leaving; most people welcome the spiritual touch.

Liz might only visit two or three people on some days, for she has to adapt her programme according to the needs which come before her each day. It is sometimes hard and unrewarding work, as it takes a long time to gain the confidence of some of these lonely people. Liz feels strongly that she has to earn the right to talk to them on deeper things by gaining their friendship first.

We leave Liz, back at home, brailling a note to a blind friend at Torch, asking her to pass on all the news and items for prayer in chapel time. Liz knows the value of a prayerful backing, and makes full use of the prayer-link with Torch House.

So, in at least one city, something is being done full-time to meet the spiritual needs of blind people in the loneliness of modern city life.

What is happening in Bristol is needed in so many other cities. Manchester, London, Glasgow—all these areas are crying out for strong Fellowship Groups, and for full-time visitation programmes. What God has done in Bristol may well be a pattern for other areas too.

CHAPTER 12—INSIDE–OUTSIDE

"What *does* go on behind those walls?" asked a passer-by, who was taking a stroll in Hallaton. "Oh, it's a convent" she was told.

People have had very strange ideas about who we are, and what we are doing. They imagine us to be cloistered serenely, apart from every-day life, "super-spiritual", or "a Home for poor blind people", or "some sort of religious factory".

To many blind people throughout the world, Torch House is home, where they can be sure of a welcome and someone with whom to share their joys and sorrows. But we are a mystery to those outside the Family. Welfare authorities cannot determine which pigeon-hole to put us in, and other official bodies are somewhat confused as to our activities.

The only way to overcome these misunderstandings is to make sure there is a two-way traffic, so that we go out and they come in.

We soon discovered we had "them" coming in uninvited, when we were visited by vandals—boys and girls from the village, who made a game of trespassing in the garden and playing in the woods. The greatest damage they did was to ram an iron rod through the plastic lining of our swimming-pool The water ran out, and the pool was useless for the rest of the season. One of the blind girls made a point of praying for the village children, especially the ones who damaged the pool! This made us more aware of the needs of the folk in the village than ever.

Apart from the village Bible study, which several of our staff attend regularly, we had very little spiritual contact with the village. So we prayed that the Lord would give us an opportunity to witness. We planned a children's mission one August, using a tent in the grounds. A number of families were staying with us in the house, and so we had a nucleus of children to work on. Several young people who couldn't manage to come at the time of the Young People's Houseparty were also with us. So we enlarged our plans, and extended invitations to the children in the villages around. They turned up in force, and over sixty gathered each morning for a session.

The first day that the mission opened, the missioner held up his Bible and asked if the children knew what it was. It became evident that many of the children had not met the Bible before, nor heard the lovely Bible stories. Hilary Smale, who was then with Bible Club Movement, helped the missioner and used flannelgraph pictures to illustrate the stories. One day she showed a picture of the story of Joseph. Next day she had a quiz. "Who was the boy who dreamed?" she asked. Quickly a boy put his hand up at the back, "The fellow in the striped T-shirt", he said with all seriousness. The workers were challenged; it was a thrill to see these children absorbing the Gospel stories for the first time. Parents were most grateful and even brought little gifts in appreciation. The weather was perfect for that first mission, and added greatly to the success of such things as Sports Day.

As a result of the mission, a Children's Club was started every Thursday evening, so that regular teaching could be given and so that the children of staff could be catered for as well. It was a very small beginning, but it was a good foundation on which to build our relationships with the village.

Some of our staff accepted responsibility for organising the evening service at the local village chapel. This opened a few more doors into the life of the village. One staff family linked up with the Parish church in the village, too, so gradually we became more integrated with the villagers.

On special occasions, such as Christmas, we have united services in the church. At such times the Torch choir is a welcome point of interest in the service. These occasions have helped further to break down the "them" and "us" attitude, and have made "the wall" seem a less formidable obstacle.

All this time the village people have been coming to the doctors' surgery in the house, where they have plenty of opportunity to see us at work. Open Days, too, give a chance for anyone outside to come in to see the work being done in the production departments.

Although the village folk are all very friendly, yet there is still a reserve to be broken through before we can really get into the heart of Hallaton village.

But there are plenty of visitors from further afield, coach-loads of people from Fellowship Groups, Mothers' Unions, churches interested in the work, and groups of welfare workers too, who are anxious to know how much we can help them. We do not reckon to provide more than a cup of tea and cake for these groups, except for those with blind people from a club or a Fellowship Group. The size of group is usually up to fifty; in fact, we tell organisers not to bring more. Imagine our shock when two days before one group was due, we learned that ninety people were coming! As it was a Fellowship Group, we didn't like to disappoint them, so we appealed to the staff for extra help. They were dears! One of them cancelled going home, others put off shopping trips, and the staff in the house shouldered the extra work with real joy. For there is a two-way blessing in these Fellowship Group visits; we can actually meet the people we help with literature and tapes, and they can get to know us personally. One lady who came in with that Group said, "I'm not going to give you my name, I don't want you to "follow me up" by contacting me, but I want you to pray for me; I'm going home to get sorted out, because I have been deeply challenged." If we had insisted on only fifty people, she might have been left behind! We have very interesting conversations with the coach drivers on these occasions too; in fact, some of our men-folk reckon to welcome them specially.

The biggest single factor which impresses these visitors is our financial policy. They see a comfortable home, and a literature and tape work going on without any capital in the bank, just a day-to-day dependence on the Lord. And as none of us look starved and deprived (some look the very opposite!) they are amazed. As we give the glory for this to God Himself, these people become very thoughtful. "Religion", as they call it, seems to work in some places after all!

When visitors come to us they often ask to hear the choir. Every Tuesday evening it is Choir Practice in the chapel. "I came in feeling absolutely done," one of the men said to me, "but in choir, when we praise the Lord like this, it makes me feel on top again!" This could be echoed by many of us as we come to choir feeling tired after a day's work, and yet have the joy of being able to praise the Lord together. Yes, we love choir!

At one time it seemed as if our choir would have to be disbanded. We did not know who could lead it, and we had no-one who could play the piano. Of course, our choir did not need to be conducted, as only half of our members could see, and it is very difficult to conduct a choir which cannot see the conductor. However, when the future seemed to be very uncertain, the Lord sent us Jill. Jill just oozes harmony, and can play a wide range of instruments, including the piano. Then Carol came, she also can play a number of instruments, and is very good at preparing manuscripts where necessary. Then the Lord started to give new songs to members of the choir. Sometimes one would have words and another the tune. Gemma was especially singled out by the Lord to receive from Him words and music. It just seemed to pour out of her, and we knew these songs were anointed of God. So we found ourselves with not only a choir, but song-writers, script-writers, and soloists as well. We also found that we had the makings of an orchestra. Men came along too, and we were able to have four-part harmony to most of the songs. The choir had come alive again.

Jill is a very gentle leader, sensitive and patient. She has made us ashamed of our rather rugged performances of the past, without even criticising them, but by showing us how much better we could be. As always, choir starts with a time of prayer, and sometimes we stop half-way to pray if a need intrudes on our minds. "In everything by prayer and supplication in the Spirit . . ." We don't drop tools and pray as a duty, it is rather an inside urge to share a new joy or problem with our beloved Lord. We are not a lot of holy angels, far from it! We occasionally have disagreements, but they don't usually last many minutes. And we have a great deal of fun!

The ministry of the choir is being blessed wherever it goes, and this is not anything to do with our ability or our holiness. I believe it is because, deep down in our hearts, we really do mean the lovely words which we sing. Opportunities to go to Clubs for the blind, or Homes for blind old people are very fulfilling, and the conversations afterwards are often rewarding. "Those songs reminded me of a tent mission I went to years ago . . . ." Memories of the past are often stirred, and we meet people who used to know the joy of salvation, but who have strayed from God, as well as some who are still wistfully searching. Here is a typical letter of thanks:—

"Thank you so much for bringing your choir to our Blind Club. I can't describe what it is, but you brought an atmosphere that was refreshing and challenging. Thank you!"

One friend of the Family was so touched by the choir's performance that he provided us with new choir clothes—the old dresses were wearing out. Then our Nottingham Torch Fellowship gave us artificial roses to brighten up our new navy and white pinafore dresses. The result was very pleasing.

Of course, we do more than sing—we introduce the songs, and intersperse them with testimonies, readings from braille, and poems. This is a form of service which we thoroughly enjoy, though at some seasons of the year we find ourselves very busy indeed.

Occasionally, the choir is asked to sing on the radio, and this is a tremendous opportunity to spread the joyous Gospel of the Lord Jesus.

So, you see, we are by no means confined behind those walls at Hallaton. I hope this chapter has helped you to appreciate that there is a healthy in-and-out, a coming-and-going, so that we should find it hard to become insular!

CHAPTER 13 — ON TOUR

When we had only twelve Fellowship Groups we had no difficulty in visiting them yearly. But as the Family grew we found it impossible to meet them all. So we started to send out teams from Hallaton to spend weekends in the neighbourhood of a Fellowship Group, and on occasions to tour an area.

It is a privilege to be welcomed by rich and poor alike. Ideal conditions do not always go with deep warm fellowship. Whether we eat from dainty china, with serviettes at the ready, or enjoy fish and chips from newspaper, our hearts are warmed when "they that love the Lord speak often one to another". We are sad at times when our conversation does not get beyond the superficial, but we can recall many glad occasions when a love-link has been shared with others who love our Lord. Mind you, very often our times of fellowship warm up at the end of a busy day, and we find ourselves involved in deep conversation long after bed-time. These are precious moments, however, when we share rich experiences with each other, and talk about our Saviour. Such fellowship compensates for the longing which comes over us sometimes: "Oh, for my own little bed!" We realise the truth of what Jesus said, that when we are willing to leave home and family for His sake, we receive much more than we might have sacrificed. How many brothers and sisters He has given us! How many of the Lord's homes have been opened wide to us. Yes, we feel very rich.

Fitting in with the customs of the house can be quite amusing. Signing the Visitors' Book is a ritual observed widely these days. A glance through it quite often brings out a talking point: "I see you had so-and-so here two years ago." "Oh, yes, he left his socks behind. All our visitors seem to leave something!" We wonder if we shall follow the same pattern! The daily reading with the family varies widely from a short hurried prayer, through lovely readings and discussions, to the extreme reached by one devout family. They read the Scripture Union portion followed by Daily Bread Notes and then Daily Light, Broken Bread and two other daily readings. To complete the devotions, five or six missionary prayer guides were produced, consulted and prayed over. We couldn't remember half of the matters discussed, but they could, and did they pray!

One loveable, absent-minded host spent a long time grouping us outside his front door for a photograph. He took several shots with his camera as he wanted to finish up the film he had used at a niece's wedding. "That's finished", he exclaimed triumphantly at last. He disappeared to unload the camera and post off the film. Next morning his wife confided to us: "I'm afraid my husband's photography has not been very successful." "Oh?" we asked. "No," she explained, "he forgot to put a film into the camera!"

A hair-raising exercise is that of "following" a car. We have to go to a church at the other end of an unfamiliar town. "Oh, I'll lead you; just you follow", our host offers. As we get into our car we wish we knew the address of the church, and could have a map, but no, we must "follow". Engines are revved up, and soon we are shooting across traffic lights at amber, missing pedestrians on crossings by inches, taking risks at road

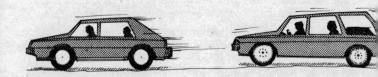

junctions and losing our bearings at roundabouts as we follow our kind 'Jehu!' At other times we have misunderstood the instructions given to us. We shall not easily forget chasing round one town for an hour trying to reach our Sunday lunch, with no address to go to, just instructions to follow "from the station." We, of course, had found our way to the wrong station!

Yes, tours have a decidedly funny side to them! What a blessing it is to have a sense of humour!

But it is almost overwhelming when you come face to face with the needs of human hearts. Oh, the heartbreak we felt for a blind man whose wife had left him—he had to ask his young children to read the legal correspondence relating to his divorce! Then the bitterness which spilled out from the man who had come home from a prisoner of war camp to find his home, wife and children bombed to bits. He lost his sight eventually and was in darkness indeed. These are some of the twice-blinded people to whom the Lord has called us.

The Homes for the blind which we visit vary a great deal. In one area we went to a Home run by the Council which had a bright cheery Christian matron who was not a bit afraid to let all the people know that she loved the Lord. What a happy place that home was. She told us that two-thirds of her staff had become Christians and many of the residents too. One word sprang to our minds, the word hope. They had a certainty, an expectancy, a hope which was eternal. What a contrast when we visited another Home in the same area. The futureless waiting for death, the moans and groans—oh, it was so depressing. One dear man in that Home was anxious to find something better. He sat all day reading the Scriptures but not understanding them. We offered to send him simple Bible studies, but he was not at all sure about them, and so he declined the offer. We could only pray for a shaft of light from the Lord to open the Word to him.

We were told of two blind people who lived in an Old People's Home which was run by a nominally Christian Society. Could we give them anything to help them spiritually? Neither of them could read any form of writing or embossed literature. Unfortunately, one of the rules of this Home was, that to avoid offending any of the residents, the name of Jesus Christ must not be mentioned. Even the playing of cassettes was disapproved of. We were not able to visit this Home, or to do anything to bring the Hope of the Gospel to these two blind people.

Visiting in some of the purpose-built flats for blind people can be very rewarding. We had a long chat with two ladies who were spiritually confused. Their "faith" was a mixture of the Jehovah's Witness teaching, and a weird "meditation" theory which had been propounded over the radio. What could we do in such a short time for such people? We could only present Christ in His loveliness, and pray that they would look to Him through their confusion. They were so grateful for our visit.

Usually the main trouble about tours is not how to get a meal, but where to put the food which is offered! Dear, kind hostesses spend hours preparing luxurious dishes with such evident love that our hearts melt. On just a few occasions, however, the time-table plays havoc with meals. At one place it was the custom to have a light sandwich lunch at midday as the family always ate their main meal in the evening. However, we were out to afternoon tea for two days in succession and so we missed the main meal for several days. At last we had to take a long journey to reach our evening engagement and couldn't find anywhere which was open for a meal. When the meeting was over we faced a forty mile drive back. We were desperately hungry, so hungry in fact that at 10.30 p.m. we patronised the fish and chip shop. None of us liked fish much, but that fish wrapped in newspaper and eaten with bare hands, tasted delicious to us. How we gave thanks for that meal!

The weather can make quite a difference to our impression of a place. I remember visits in the pouring rain more than in the sunshine. One day on our way to Norwich in driving rain we saw what looked like a paper bag floating in a puddle in the road. Suddenly the "paper bag" showed itself to be a duck! We had to take swift evasive action. Norwich is a beautiful city and well merits the description which it proudly displays:

"Norwich, a fine city", but it greeted us with rain, rain, rain! However, our fellowship with the Torch Family in Norwich was really fine!

One Winter the enemy was snow. For several months Fellowships as far apart as Yorkshire and Wales had to cancel meetings. We tried to go to every engagement we had arranged, and slithered to a stop outside deserted halls to find that the weather had caused last-minute cancellations. On one such trip, we became snowed-out and could not return to Hallaton when we'd planned to do so, as all the roads into Hallaton were blocked by snow. However, these trials were all temporary ones, and made us realise how much we should value every opportunity given to us to preach the Gospel.

Once we went through an absolute downpour to a preliminary Fellowship meeting; it was held in a mission for down-and-outs which was beautifully painted and lovingly cared for. However, we had an unusual company that night, a guide-dog which kept taking our hats and gloves and playing with them on the floor, a down-and-out sheltering from the rain, and a very cheeky inquisitive mouse! This was an odd assortment with which to start a new work, but the Lord moved the people in that area, and a Fellowship Group was started.

On deputation trips we are likely to meet with alarmingly temperamental equipment, like geysers which seem to explode diabolically when they are lit. We can find ourselves in damp or uncomfortable beds, and noisy neighbourhoods. Once we were awakened rudely by hooters and loud speakers at 7 a.m. Sometimes we are greeted by the little children of the household visiting us early in the morning. But we have shared many homes which are full of love, and where fellowship is so sweet! Yes, in spite of minor physical discomforts at times, we hold a store of treasured memories where Christ Himself has been so real, that our hearts have "burned within us" as we have talked of Jesus with His children.

Everywhere that we have visited, we have been made conscious of the needs of blind people around us. On one occasion, when we were in London, we met a woman who was so worried about being blind that she did not dare to dress herself, but stayed in bed all day. She was greatly helped by a blind member of our team who gave her tips on how to dress herself 'in the dark'.

The ideal team for visitation of this sort is a sighted person working with a visually handicapped partner. A blind mother, with two young children, had refused to see the local City Missionary when he called, so he asked the team to visit her. She opened the door. "Are any of you blind?" she asked. "Yes, I am" came the reply. "Come in", she said, "you're one of us!"

Unfortunately, we were not able to find any local Christians who could take up the challenge and continue to visit her. The lack of interest among sighted Christians is very disheartening. Most blind folk are anxious to have help; many welfare officers are only too glad to support any effort made; but on the whole Christians seem to be indifferent to the need.

Finding the way can be quite an experience in deputation work. Sue was due at a meeting at 2.30 p.m. She had toured round and round in the car, but at 2.20 p.m. she still couldn't find out how to reach the hall where the meeting was to be held. She stopped, threw the map down on the floor of the car: "I just can't find it!" she exclaimed. Her companion suggested that they prayed. At that moment, a Police car drew up in front of them. Sue ran out and asked the police how to get to the place of the meeting. "Follow us, my dear, we'll get you there in time", they replied. Sure enough, just before 2.30 p.m. they rolled up outside the hall!

Ken was sent with Penny to a meeting in South Ealing. They committed the meeting and journey to the Lord and then, in darkness and heavy rain, they started the journey across London. There seemed to be too many dazzling car lights, such a lot of dim road signs, and far too much traffic as they headed west. Through Lambeth and Chelsea, they followed the river. Then they came to a one-way system and lost their sense of direction! Suddenly a sign greeted them: "London Airport." Feeling sure he had gone too far, Ken drew up in to a lay-by beside a brightly-lit garage. It was still raining hard, so he dashed inside to ask the way. The garagemen pointed to a nearby turning, which was the one he needed to take! Wiping the raindrops from his eyebrows, Ken drove on, grateful to the Lord that he would not have to try to make a 'U' turn, a difficult manoeuvre in London traffic. Some people might think this was just coincidence, but Ken and his passenger knew that it was not!

In 1973 we made our first visit to Northern Ireland. We arrived at the Belfast docks in the grey light of a February morning to find the Province paralysed by a strike.

"No buses to-day!" — "Our poor little country." — "What will become of us?" These were some of the remarks which we overheard as we sat waiting for the arrival of our escort.

He came, on time, the one smiling face in the whole glum scene. "What are the prospects of our tour?" we asked. "No problem—no problem at all" he replied cheerfully.

His optimism affected us, and we began to take fresh heart. Consequently, we had a wonderful tour. We visited schools, churches, homes and, best of all, the Belfast Torch Fellowship Group, the only one in Northern Ireland at that time. We enjoyed rich warm Fellowship all around. The Irish have the reputation of being fiery; we certainly found them warm—with love.

Our second visit to Ireland was during another strike—we obviously had a bad effect on the political scene! It was evident that feeling was running high. Groups of young people and older men lounged around, unable to work. Very few buses were running, factories were closed, shops only opened for half days. Meat was "subject to delivery", bread too was not easy to procure. And worse, we detected a defeated and dejected downward look in our dear fellow Christians. Temporarily their troubles had over-shadowed their faith—understandably. We could not judge them; they had been worn down by constant tension and violence. But just a few of the saints were filled with spiritual optimism.

The first Houseparty of the Belfast Torch Fellowship was due to be held from the Friday night to the Sunday night at Bangor.

"Human road-block isolates Bangor", we read. "Petrol strictly rationed; no more supplies can get through", and so it went on.

"We must cancel the Houseparty" said one of the Committee. But the blind people involved were *longing* for a chance to drink deeply of the Water of Life—they were mostly from the troubled parts of Belfast and were starved for want of fellowship.

Welfare buses were laid on to take people down to Bangor, but at the last minute they were withdrawn because of the situation. No wonder the organiser of the Houseparty cried "Whatever shall we do?"

But we saw courage and faith at work. "That's no problem. I'll lay on transport", said one—and he did! Others, following his lead, made great sacrifices to take the blind folk to Bangor for the Conference.

We lost count of the number of problems presented to us during our stay in Ireland, but each one was surmounted.

It is true! Civil strife may take us unawares, but it never surprises our Sovereign Lord. It is no problem to Him. If only we could all have trust and love, and reliance on God as some of our friends in Northern Ireland had that time.

The Bangor Houseparty was a tremendous blessing,

although we wondered at the beginning if we should get anywhere at all! At that first meal, our Irish family sat with ears glued to the radio which was pouring out propaganda, gloomy prognoses, arguments for and against. To us, the uninitiated, it was all a bewildering mass of words. We suggested that the radio be left upstairs for two days so that the Voice of God could be heard, and not the words of man. Our dear friends saw the point, and we had no more radios at meal times. At first, everyone seemed so weighed down, that even the singing was poor. But the Lord just poured in His love and joy, until every heart was touched. Some came to know Jesus as Saviour, some tasted His love in a new way, others claimed His power to live in difficult circumstances. Gradually we saw their faces change as they began to relax and enjoy the peace of God which passes understanding!

When we start out on a tour, or to speak at a Conference, or in any way to break new ground, we feel a sense of responsibility and a thrill of expectancy. Who knows how many people will be brought into a closer relationship with Christ, or how many will find a new satisfaction in serving Him? And how many who are twice-blind will receive the Light of Life in their hearts?

As a family we are glad of all opportunities to go out into the regions. On some weekends as many as five groups are out visiting Torch Fellowship Groups, singing, etc. and so meeting a widening circle of friends.

This type of ministry can be very exciting, but the team has to be ready for any service which might present itself.

"School assembly on Monday, girls. Okay?" The girls wished they had brought more young people's hand-out literature, yet their cases were bulging as it was! Outwardly calm, they replied: "Yes, we'll be ready!" Or it may be, "I've asked the man to come from Local Radio to interview you. I hope you don't mind." They love to be ready to speak out for the Lord at any time.

The planning behind all these visits takes place at the "Diary Committee". Before we start to look at the letters asking us to visit any area, we spend a time in prayer. Does the

Lord want us to go? Would accepting that invitation stretch our resources too much? Just as the Lord directed Paul to Macedonia and opened up Europe to the Gospel, so He can direct us to-day. It is vital that we pray over all our deputation meetings and tours.

We thoroughly enjoy visiting a church "in depth". For this we usually take a team of six so that we can speak to the Sunday School, the Bible Classes, take morning and evening worship, and finally have time to go into things even more fully in an after-church Fellowship. In this way Christians gain deeper insight into the many aspects of the work of Torch. It is surprising how often people have said, "I thought I knew all about Torch! But I can see I knew very little." There is another benefit too, for as the Church members entertain the team, they get to know them more intimately. Many lovely friendships have been formed in this way. It is a great reward to us when, as a result of such a visit, people discover how they can help their own blind neighbours.

However, there is a subtle danger to spiritual well-being which we have to guard against when "On Tour". It comes with a two-pronged action. One prong which catches us unawares, is the "praise of men". Sometimes, humans and their gifts are glorified instead of the Lord. This nasty prong has a special way of singling out blind people. "Oh, you're just wonderful. That singing! That playing!" This approach is so obviously the praise of men that it must be received with humility and handed back to the Lord who gave every talent in the first place. But this type of compliment can come dressed up in spiritual clothing. "Oh, that message—you have a real gift . ..!" Here it has to be distinguished between the genuine heart-felt thanks of a person who has been blessed by the Lord, and one whose motive is to flatter. It depends what we do when we receive such words. If we get a little puffed up, then we are in danger. We need at such times to look at John 15 and acknowledge, "Without Me ye can do nothing". Above all, we have to have a single purpose in our work. If we speak to try to get audience-response (very tempting for a blind speaker) before long we find ourselves seeking the praise of men and, like the fear of men, it becomes a snare.

The second "prong" of the enemy's attack concerns our quiet time. Strange beds sometimes mean disturbance of sleep-pattern, and kind hosts and hostesses encourage us to "lie in for a bit". This is welcome, but it is so easy to get up later, and become involved in a round of activity, without that vital time with the Lord. "Oh, I'll only have a short Bible reading to-day; I'll make up for it later on." Unfortunately, "later on" doesn't come. The result of this is not seen immediately but, gradually, if we are on a longer tour, we begin to show that we have not had that deep vital daily infilling. Our vessels become very dry, service and counselling become automatic, and before we know where we are, we have lost our first love. The fact that this condition is not apparent straight away makes its approach so insidious, and the result so devastating, for others notice it before we do.

"You seem to be very agitated to-day"—"Are you cross with me?" are two remarks which have brought me back to first things. If it goes to the extreme, it means that our life is open to sin, our advice to others is twisted, and our oneness with other believers is damaged.

The Church is glad to welcome people who travel around exercising a ministry of evangelism, teaching or ministering to minority groups, but the Church doesn't always realise how much the travellers need prayer. We have seen itinerant servants of God who have been wrecked by the adulation of the crowds, and the lack of time alone with God. Visiting speakers certainly need the prayers of the Church!

But pitfalls and humour apart, there is a need for Christians to share their faith, their burdens, and their work. Yes, it is obvious that we still need to go "On Tour".

CHAPTER 14 — ALL OVER THE WORLD

When the tiny magazine "Torch" began its wanderings in 1931 a number of missionaries asked to have it to give to blind people under their care. It found its way to several countries, including China and India, where blind people had been taught English braille in Christian schools. But because of political upheavals, the retirement of missionaries, and the fact that in some cases the English language was not taught any more, over the years some of these overseas links were broken.

However, more recently, a new urge to learn on the part of young people in the third world has brought a spate of braille letters asking for something to read and for simple Bible studies. Gradually, the number of overseas readers of our magazines has increased. These facts made us begin to feel an increasing burden for the blind of the world. India, we learned, has nine million visually handicapped people; there are a quarter of a million blind Arabs; Nigeria has one million blind, and river blindness in Ghana has left whole villages without a fully sighted person. All these people need the Gospel message, and need something to read which will help them to grow in Christ.

We wondered what was being done to meet the special needs of the blind by the Christian Church. The Lutheran Church had a braille programme, and we knew of other societies who were publishing a limited amount of braille literature. The Gospel Association for the Blind and the Braille Circulating Library in America, and the Christian Foundation for the Blind in Australia—all were doing their bit. But it was difficult to get a clear picture of the scope of Christian activity for the blind. Surely, we thought, someone ought to marshall information so that those with resources to spare could help those who had none.

We took a look at our own programme, and the contacts which we had. Almost all of our association with overseas was through the distribution of Christian literature in braille. However, we had one or two personal contacts with folk who were working with blind people. A blind Nepali Christian, a teacher at a school for the blind, came to this country to take an educational course in Edinburgh. He became a regular visitor to the Edinburgh Torch Fellowship. "I must start a Torch Fellowship Group when I get back to Kalimpong" he said. Sure enough, he did. Blind people who go to the Kalimpong Torch Fellowship sit cross-legged on a veranda as they sing choruses, and listen to the message of the Gospel. The language, of course, is different but the fellowship is the same. From that Fellowship Group, another group was formed at Cooch-bihar. This was a very small beginning, when we think of the many who need to hear the Gospel, but it was a start. One member of that Fellowship Group was in the habit of meeting a blind beggar every day. He felt a great urge to tell the beggar about Jesus. Eventually, he went up to him and said, "Jesus Christ loves you. He died for you to make you His child." The beggar was amazed. Someone loving a beggar? "Why didn't anyone tell me this before?" he asked. He gave his poor life to the Lord, and after very little more teaching, he went on his way. Later, he was traced five hundred miles away. He couldn't read but he could sing, so he made up songs about the love of Jesus, and sang them to the crowds. He was drawing people to the Saviour by his testimony in song.

Our links were strong with Bangladash too. We knew Veronica Campbell when she worked as a Social Worker for the blind before going abroad. It seemed natural that when Bangladesh gained its independence, Veronica should be involved in helping the blind of that country. She translated Scriptures giving the story of the life and death of our Lord Jesus Christ into Bengali braille, and we had the joy of producing it for her. It was proof-read by some Muslim university students, and it made a profound impression upon them. They wanted to follow the call of Christ—but so much stood in the way! However, several young blind people did give their hearts to the Lord, and a Fellowship Group was started. There are two now in Bangladesh, one in the centre of Dacca which attracts blind men and women, and one in the suburbs which is mainly for young men.

We have very happy links too with blind people in Sweden. We visited Sweden in 1975 linking on with "Sysconbandet", a Swedish blind association with similar fellowship aims to Torch. We visited a number of churches, and told the Christians of the need to reach blind people with the Gospel. We also visited a Training Centre for younger blind folk, who were keen to try out their English. A number of folk in Sweden began to take our magazines, and there was considerable interest in holding a joint Anglo-Swedish Houseparty.

Apart from these areas in which we had a personal interest,

we had only scant knowledge of Christian activity amongst the blind overseas, through the requests which reached us for literature.

It was Jose, a young blind Spaniard, who first raised the idea of an International Conference, to find out what was being done world-wide to meet the need. He was one of those young blind men with a vision.

"If we could only get together," Jose said, "surely a lot more could be done!" Jose did his best to encourage us to host a Conference at Hallaton. Our friends in Australia, Pearl and Peter Sumner, and Graham Laycock, also had a vision for some world-wide assessment of the situation. So we found ourselves involved in the planning of "Hallaton '76".

It was the year of the heat-wave, and as we sat in sessions in our little Chapel, we were so hot that even our friends from Africa felt "warm".

"I'll have something to say to my friends when I get home", one of the Australian delegates said. "They told me to bring woollies because the English weather is so bad. That means I've only got one summer dress. Imagine wearing woollies in this heat!"

Day after day the sun shone from a cloudless sky, and gradually England's green and pleasant land became brown and dry. But the delegates enjoyed it all. Nineteen nations were represented by about fifty delegates. Some came from countries with a high standard of living, others from poorer circumstances. There could have been flashpoints, as Arabs from Israel conversed with Arabs from Jordan and Lebanon, and both East and West Germany were represented. However, they were all so united in their desire to spread the Gospel that there was no friction. Mr. Fouad Nasir from the Lebanon School for the Blind had a remarkable experience getting away from war-torn Lebanon to attend the Conference; Janet Claycombe "happened" to arrive at London Airport with a party of orphans from Korea, and so was able to come to Hallaton to represent the work there. Bitrus and Amose Gani from Nigeria made a delightful and colourful contribution to the discussions. Daniele from

France was fascinated to feel Bitrus' curly hair! Lars-Ove Arnesson from Sweden and other friends from Japan, Switzerland, Spain and France all mingled together in very lovely fellowship.

The Christoffel Blindenmission were represented by Dr. and Mrs. Schulze. Mr. Stein, who is in charge of their international division was able to pay a flying visit to the conference. Their work amongst the visually handicapped is very practical and educational.

In the cool of the day they would gather under the cedar tree and sing. Bitrus would lead choruses, and Jose would play and sing to delight us all. The main language used was English. Daniele translated all the talks and discussions into French, which was better understood by delegates from Switzerland and Spain. One of the East German delegates could be seen sitting out in the sunshine early each morning, translating some of the Conference literature into German for her friend, Pastor Peter Bendin, also from East Germany. It was good to see everyone making an effort to communicate; it reduced the language barrier considerably.

The talks began with reports of the activities of the various societies represented. This helped us all to know what was available at present. Braille presses where evangelical literature was produced were few. There was a very active all-purpose press in Japan which produced Christian and educational material. Korea was just starting to set up a press, and there were plans to have one in India also.

We shared with the delegates the evident hunger we had found for Braille Christian literature, and read letters from Burma, Ethiopia, Ghana and Nigeria, Sarawak, the Himalayas and even from China. A letter from Rhodesia summed them up. "Keep supplying books; don't stop them coming. They help us and others who listen when we read them aloud in our villages. They preach God's words; that is why the people appreciate them."

There was obviously a need to print more braille literature, especially in the national languages worldwide. We ourselves felt challenged by the needs of Europe which is geographically so close to us. Many blind people in Spain are obliged to sell lottery tickets in order to make a living. Senor Padilla of Nueva Luz has taken up the burden of need there, and is using radio and tapes to bring the Gospel to blind Spanish-speaking people. It was thrilling to hear first-hand of his vision, and to share his difficulties too.

Monique Durleman of La Cause and Daniele Bueche and M. and Mme. Kunzie told us of the situation with French braille, and the openings they have for it in Africa as well as in Europe.

Our friends in East and West Germany and Holland were better placed, for they had established libraries and Fellowship Groups which were adequately meeting the needs of German readers. There was very little to report in other Eastern European countries, though we did know of a little group working in Poland.

During the Conference we split into geographical groups for practical discussion. Those from the southern hemisphere, Europe, the Middle East, America and Japan were able to discuss ways in which they could help each other. One result of this was that an acceptable translation and braille code was approved, so that the Bible could be produced in Arabic braille. Eventually a young blind Arab named Hanna came to stay at Torch house for three months to braille an "original"

113

for the Acts of the Apostles in Arabic braille. This was a direct outcome of the discussion groups with the delegates from the Middle East. We also undertook to braille a French Scripture Text Calendar for the Mission Evangelique Braille, and were able to welcome Maria from Spain, first for a holiday stay, then later to teach her the whole of our braille system so that, after a Bible College training, she could go back to Spain fully equipped to set up a press there. Eventually, we also had the joy of having Birendra Rongong with us, who embossed St. John's Gospel in Nepali braille for us to print.

Altogether, Hallaton '76 was a revelation and a challenge. The outstanding feature was the deep fellowship which developed during the ten days of the Conference. We were all one in purpose, that of bringing the Light of the Gospel to the twice-blind of the world. In the prayer meetings delegates would pray in their own languages and, during our time of communion on Sunday morning, we all united to pray the prayer taught by our Lord to His disciples, each in his own language. "Our Father, ... " How wonderful it is that each language is known to God, and in each country there are those who can truly call Him Father because they have been born again into His family. In the warm, light evenings as we gathered under the cedar tree to sing the songs which are loved by the Christian Church all over the world, the barriers of race and language seemed so small.

There were several other practical results of Hallaton '76. One has been the founding of "Christ for the Blind International", and the publication of a newsletter which is a report of events and advances being made in the realm of Christian activity for the blind. This report is compiled and printed by us at Torch. Mike Townsend is the editor. Also, as a result of Hallaton '76 Roger Mundy, who was the main organiser for the Conference, compiled a monumental "Directory" of all Christian activities for the blind world-wide. This directory is invaluable, and avoids overlapping in one area and under-development in another.

It never ceases to amaze us the way the world comes to us at Hallaton. Our literature goes out now to over sixty different countries, and it is requested in increasing quantities. Also, we have visitors who come to us from all over the world. Earlier on we had Dawn from Canada, Nabil from Egypt, Shahim from Iran, Francoise and Rosemarie from Germany, Ivy and Lee from Singapore, Christo from South Africa, Febe and Annicke from Sweden, Glen from U.S.A., Lars from Sweden, Miss Bray from New Zealand, Cephas from Nigeria, Danny from Korea, not to mention the number of flying visits made by Tony and Rona Gibb, who are helping to set up Fellowship Centres in India where, among other things, they are distributing braille literature to some of the 20,000 blind people in their part of India who can read braille.

So, year by year, we are finding very precious love links with the people of God all over the world, and especially with those who are blind. We have treasured memories of their visits to us, and who knows, maybe we shall be visiting them before the Lord returns.

CHAPTER 15 — WORDS, WORDS, WORDS!

What a mess!

The Editorial room floor was littered with papers, pens, scissors and magazines. There were pages torn from Christian periodicals, glue, several different versions of the Bible, reference books, and even a few people! An Editorial Committee was in progress. Barbara was digesting articles from Christian publications; Gemma, with the use of her visual aid, was deep in a Bible study; Eileen was laboriously counting words, and I was writing an editorial for "Channels of Blessing". "Channels" is a braille magazine issued by the Royal National Institute for the Blind, but edited by us. It is mainly a digest of articles from the Christian Press and is a real challenge to edit. We have to literally pull print magazines to pieces to provide the articles needed for it!

We had already begun our Committee with a lovely time of prayer—something which we always do before any editorial work. The reading, writing and counting continued. There was a companionable silence, broken occasionally by remarks such as: "Can I read you this bit?"—"I'm not sure that I've put this the right way round." — "This is a good article; would you like to come and listen?" — "I think we have chosen too many missionary features. We want something devotional now." — "Have you collected the news items yet? People really do want to know what is going on in the Christian world."

Sighted friends will find it hard to realise the importance of the news column in a braille publication. Many blind people have no other contact with Christian literature and no-one to read print magazines to them.

"Moon Messenger" offers a similar, but possibly even greater challenge than "Channels". Like "Channels", it is a digest, but it is published monthly in Moon type. This Moon type is not easily produced as it requires specially cast type, and dampened paper to make the embossing. It is only printed in one place in the world, the R.N.I.B. Moon Branch at Reigate, Surrey. Editing "Moon Messenger" is a great responsibility as there is so little Christian literature in Moon type. We have to choose material for the mature Christian, yet we must also think of readers who have not committed their lives to Christ. The new Christians need to be encouraged and fed. Most Moon readers read very slowly so it is advisable to have material without complicated sentence construction. Shorter articles fit the bill, but they must be interesting and encouraging; it is no use just hammering home hard, cold facts! It is gratifying to see how much our readers appreciate their magazine; we soon hear if their copies go astray! Often "Moon Messenger" provides the only spiritual point in an otherwise empty life. An elderly lady asked her friend to write to us as she could not manage to write herself. "Thank you so much for your magazine. I am so glad I learned the 'Moon'. Before, I had nothing to do, now I can fill my days with reading the magazines you send. It has made it worth going on living again."

The other nine magazines which begin life in the Editorial room are all published by Torch, some in braille, some in large print, some in Moon and others on tape. The "Torch" magazine itself is produced in all these media.

This family magazine was a parent to all the others, and before the Editorial Department was formed, it was written solely by me. It has by far the highest circulation, and we have no idea of the number of readers, because a single magazine may be read by as many as ten people.

What strange places this little magazine reaches! In 1972 we had a letter from a missionary in Borneo. When visiting his scattered flock in the jungle, he had come to a village where there were two blind men. They had one tiny precious braille magazine between them, a very old, battered copy of "Torch", which they treasured and read out loud regularly to their fellow-villagers. The missionary wrote to enquire whether we still supplied literature, what our organisation was, and whether he would be eligible to receive something for these blind folk. Incidentally, although not blind himself, he had learned braille whilst he was held as a prisoner-of-war in a school for the blind. His captors considered it unnecessary for the school to have artificial light so, to while away the evenings, he had learned braille.

It was only after the move to Hallaton that we became an Editorial Department. Now Gemma, Barbara, Sheila and I work together on literature production. Writing for the magazines probably takes the greatest amount of our time. It is so important that every word counts. Because braille takes up so much room, we have to keep our material short and to the point. This means that we cannot often take complete articles from print magazines. Barbara, lovingly nick-named "Chief Whip", is the one who organizes us, and tells us when we have to cut down our articles to a suitable length. She is also responsible for seeing that the appropriate material is transcribed or recorded, and that it finds its way to the next stage of its life in the Production Department. It is hard to realise how we managed before she joined us in 1974. Gemma and Sheila have the laborious task of brailling and typing the articles. When they are away we realise the volume of work they get through! Their work frequently entails brailling and typing an article several times as the script is often substantially edited at a magazine committee. They both do their share of writing too.

Other members of the family join us for the editing of "Spark" the children's magazine. Some, who have a special love for the deaf-blind, help with the writing of "Our Mag". Those with missionary experience and interest work on "Link" for overseas readers. In fact, any member of the family who has a particular interest and aptitude, is encouraged to contribute. The only condition is that the writer must be thick-skinned! It is no use writing if you are not prepared to have your articles "carved-up" — in love, of course! Magazine committees are great times of fellowship and heart-searching, and we often learn a lot ourselves as we search the Scriptures together.

Each magazine caters for a specific need or age group. The first 'baby' of "Torch" was "Flash", our young people's magazine. Incidentally, its name was decided on as we were running through a thunderstorm with a blind teacher from Bethlehem! "Flash" is produced in braille, large print and is recorded on cassette. It finds its way into many schools for the blind and partially-sighted. The young people from Jordanstown School in Belfast greeted us indignantly on one of our visits: "Where are our 'Flashes'?" they demanded. They had not had them for some months. The problem was solved when it was realised that the young lady to whom the magazines were sent had left the school. She had forwarded her new address, but had not given instructions about the magazines for the school.

At another school, an eleven year-old boy kept all his copies of both "Flash" and "Spark". He read them avidly to his friends, many of whom became readers themselves. With their help, he started a school Torch library, using our booklets and magazines.

"Spark", the 'baby' of "Flash", had a rather lovely beginning. It all started when a little blind girl of eight phoned us from her school. "Hello", she said brightly. "Have you got any books and magazines to tell us about Jesus? The big children have got some, but we want some as well." A children's magazine! We had often considered it, but we had said: "We'll do something about it when we've got more experienced staff, or more time." But how could we ignore a plea like that from this little girl? Jesus said: "Suffer the little children to come to Me"; we must not be the ones to stand in their way. So, "Spark" was born! Now we have a very precious link with that girl and her family. Through her loss of sight, and the change in her when she came to know the Lord Jesus, both her parents came to know Him too. Nowadays the Lord Jesus is using them to help others with similar problems.

"Spark" is available in braille and in lower-case large print. Like "Flash" it received a warm welcome in the schools. Many Bible stories and some of the serial characters became well-loved by the children. Visually handicapped Sunday School teachers have found "Spark" very useful too.

It was clear to us by 1971 that our deaf-blind members of the family had a special need for a magazine of their own. Reading is one of the best ways of giving information and Bible teaching to the deaf-blind. But how could we possibly write for the deaf-blind? Special skills were needed to keep the language simple and yet avoid being childish or repetitive. As we prayed about this need, two well-loved friends came to mind, David and Betty Davies of South East London. They were both deaf-blind themselves, although David had a little sight. They were proficient at braille, and were known and loved in the world of the deaf-blind. Most important, they loved the Lord Jesus deeply. We had grand fellowship with

Torch House,
Hallaton.

Ron and Stella
Heath.

Hallaton Village.

The Trench sisters
Winscales House.

Torch family communion service.

Houseparty fun.

The Torch family singers.

The central committee meeting.

Magazine editing.

Computers— exciting possibilities.

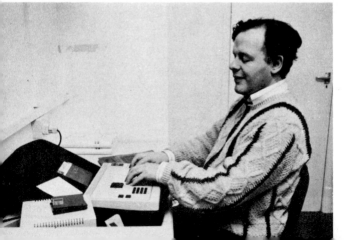

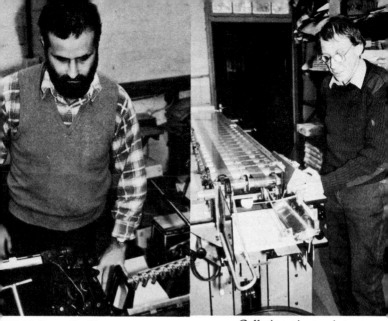

Heidelberg Braille press.

Collating giant print
literature.

The giant print library.

Recording and reading the word of life.

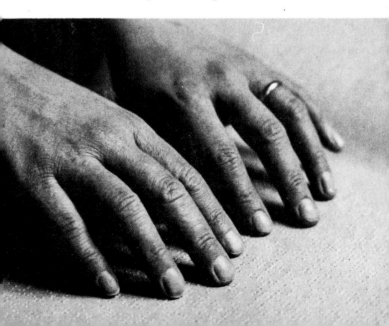

Open day, Hallaton.

Christian service training lecture.

Fleckney manor student visiting.

"Little Torch" Hurstpierpoint.

New bungalows at Hallaton

them until, in the Summer of 1973, David was knocked down and killed. Betty died not many months later. They have no need of braille now, we rejoice to say, for they are with the Lord. Now the Lord has called others here on the staff to take up the work which Betty and David did.

"Torch Times", a magazine for the thoughtful reader, was first published in December 1971 after a small literature conference had been held at Torch House, Hurstpierpoint the previous January. It became apparent that there was no suitable literature among our publications which could help blind friends with some of the questions and doctrines of the Christian faith. For years we had met with blind people who had the most strange ideas about God. Sometimes they would talk for hours, putting forward theories about God which were far removed from the truths of Scripture. When we questioned them as to how they had formulated their strange ideas, they usually said that it was from listening to programmes on the radio. It was not their fault that they did not know the truth about God and the Bible. They had never been in a position to read scholarly evangelical literature and to think the questions through from a Biblical viewpoint.

Peter Wootton, William Espejo and Rona were the original "Torch Times" Committee. Right from the start they had great times of fellowship as they edited. The committees were often held in the comfort of either Peter's or William's homes. The committee has changed inevitably over the years, but the fellowship is still very precious.

Some articles are specially written for this magazine by Bible College lecturers who have given generously of their precious time to write for us. Not everyone on the committee always agrees with every article, but providing each writer writes from one of the accredited evangelical standpoints, he "gets a hearing".

Each issue contains five or six articles apart from the Editorial and book reviews. We try to keep a balance between doctrinal, ethical, missionary and devotional articles. We have always been very conscious that the readership of this magazine includes those who have been well-taught

Christians for many years, yet also we know that some readers are new Christians, and those who have no faith, but only a critical approach to the magazine. Our main aim is to inform and teach the Christian, but we must never lose sight of the non-Christian readers.

Once, in the early days, Rona asked a lecturer if he would write an article for us. He said that he had no time as he was working on a new book. Out of interest he asked: "What kind of people read this magazine?" He settled back in his chair as Rona told him about the people who read "Torch Times". He was shocked to know that there was no other similar publication in braille; surprised to learn of the number of blind professional people, and amazed to discover that many of the basic Christian books which he took for granted were just not available to the visually handicapped. Before long he was planning eagerly how he might write a series of four articles to cover New Testament content and criticism. He had talked himself into it! Rona smiled gratefully as she left him—just one more friend who had seen something of the need and responded to it.

We came across another need through correspondence with senior scholars and young blind people who were in training. They wanted something thought-provoking yet not quite so long and involved as "Torch Times". The result is our latest addition to the magazine family, "Searchlight". This is a quarterly magazine and has articles on some of the current problems facing young people, as well as reviews and other items of interest. We produce this in braille and on cassette. It has been received with open arms by the more thoughtful young readers.

Not only is the Editorial room the birth-place of all the braille, moon, large print and recorded material which we produce or edit at Torch House—some print literature has a place in the Editorial programme too. The quarterly "Torch Family News" and the Prayer Bulletin inform our friends about what the Lord is doing through and for Torch. Children and young people come into the programme as well. Through a Scripture Union Sunday School lesson in December 1974, letters began to pour in from young people enquiring about Torch work and how they could be involved. As a result, print leaflets were prepared for the young folk to read, giving hints about how NOT to treat the visually handicapped, and suggesting ways in which young people could help the Torch Family. It has made a useful contribution to a number of Sunday School projects. Shawls and knee rugs have been passed on to elderly blind people, knitted by energetic readers. Used postage stamps have been collected too, and many precious little gifts have come from young people.

Our print literature has been made much more attractive by the coming of Paul and Jill Ferraby. Jill types originals for off-set printing, Paul designs the illustrations, and his excellent photographs make the literature "come alive".

Young braille readers overseas are very keen to learn all they can. Sometimes they have no Bibles to refer to, so they have been encouraged to earn their own Bible volumes by studying with the Scripture Gift Mission "Young Searchers Bible Study Course". When they have answered a question set on each chapter in the New Testament, they are awarded a Bible volume as a prize. These students write very interesting letters. We usually know when a boat has arrived because of the numbers of braille packages which come in the post.

We found it necessary too to provide Bible study courses for adults. The Bible Training Institute, Glasgow, and the London Bible College correspondence courses were chosen and put into braille. These courses are proving a means whereby blind people can train for Christian service. Two blind men have already trained for the ministry in this way, and one or two others are studying with similar goals in mind. But it is not necessary to have any such high aim in view. One lady in her seventies worked through several courses so that she could understand her Bible better. John Sharp of "Little Torch" is the tutor responsible for marking these courses. One of our first students was a deaf-blind lady. She had such strange ideas about God, and her active mind was always questing for the truth. We spent hours answering her letters and trying to put the Gospel clearly to her. In the end we introduced her to the London Bible College courses. She raced ahead, hungry for knowledge, and gradually the Holy Spirit revealed the truth to her. She was taken to be with the Lord very suddenly in the middle of a course. We were so glad that the Lord had met with her in time.

Now perhaps you can imagine some of the activities which take place in the Editorial room! It is like the "Cook-house" where we try to prepare food for our spiritually hungry family of visually handicapped people.

CHAPTER 16 — HELLO TORCH FAMILY!

Words are strange things. They can convey a message clear and strong, or they can seem just a jumble of meaningless letters. Wrong meanings can be read into them too. Yet words are a precious means of communication. How often at the end of the day have we relaxed with an interesting book, or been challenged to greater effort by an article in a magazine? Sometimes I have tried to imagine what it would be like if suddenly I was unable to read anything. A richness would go from my life, and I would have to find some other way of feeding my mind. Devotional reading and Bible study would go too—I should feel very much like a castaway on a desert island—without even a book!

Many people lose their sight each year, and are deprived of reading. These are the folk who benefit mostly from the recorded ministry of the Torch Family. Their letters of appreciation are precious—letters like this: "I was sitting on my bed listening. Tears were running down my cheeks—that story was just how *I* felt. You all help me so much spiritually. I wish I had met you before for I am hungry!"

Some people play a book or a magazine as many as six times so that its message can reach right into their hearts. Readers range from the very elderly, right through to the very young. Many have had to face tragedy and pain. A Friar wrote and told us that he was blind and had a terminal illness which made him unable to sleep. So, through the night he listened to our recordings and found that they lifted him to the Lord. Many readers suffer from multiple sclerosis. Some of our blind friends live alone, others are in homes, and some, like the Friar, live in communities. Younger people enjoy listening as a change from reading braille, though good braille readers still prefer to read by touch at their own pace. Some young folk have other handicaps which prevent them from learning braille. Recordings are important for them, as they have no other way of reading Bible stories and good literature for themselves. Blind housewives listen as they do the ironing, or while they are feeding the baby. All of them have come to know and love the voices of the staff as they introduce the magazines with: "Hello Torch Family".

Come and take a look behind the scenes in the recording studios. This expensive equipment and these studios all have a story to tell of the love and provision of the Lord. It has taken several years to establish the system, eliminate the bottlenecks, and to find out how to produce a really good copy. We are still researching, still replacing worn-out machines and experimenting with tapes. We are still striving to record and produce even better, clearer recordings.

The recording studios which we use were once "above-ground" air-raid shelters. They were originally apart from the house, but we have built an extension room which connects them to each other and to the house. These shelters were cold and damp and were used as paint sheds when we moved in, yet they were well-built with brick walls and thick concrete roofs. They make ideal studios now that they are lined and air-conditioned. The electricity supply is filtered too to eliminate hums and buzzes, which can spoil the recording and copying. The recording studio is in the centre of the complex, with a smaller control room at one side. A treble-glazed window in the wall makes it possible for the operator to see what is going on in the studio. The floors are covered with special carpet tiles and the studio walls are lined to produce the right sound effect.

A magazine is just being recorded. Several of our staff have very good recording voices and they are waiting with their scripts in braille and print. A reading desk has been specially constructed for braille readers so that no sound is picked up as their fingers slide over the dots. Chris is speaking: "Now, don't forget, if you make a blunder when you are reading—stop, then go back to the beginning of the sentence and start again. Don't do it too often though!" Most of the readers from the staff are used to recording, but any newcomers find this waiting-time very trying. "Relax, don't worry—now let's have a voice test to get the levels right." As we leave them to it, we know that each one is praying not only for the ability to put the right expression into his own part, but for the magazine as a whole, and for that invisible audience to whom it is going.

When that recording has been completed, it will be edited and handed into the third air-raid shelter which has been divided into three booths. Here several helpers, blind and sighted, work at the task of copying the magazines, and putting them into bags ready for the post. They also help with copying the Scriptures, preparing Scripture Union portions, and copies of books. Ralph was one of those whom the Lord brought along just at the right time to help us in this department. We were in need of a good, careful operator for cassette copying at that time, someone who could carry out routine copying and yet keep an ear open for faults. In a Tape Department meeting one morning we prayed for the right man to come forward as the demands for cassettes were snowballing. In the evening Ralph came on a visit. He said: "If there is any way in which I can help I shall be pleased to do it." He knew nothing of our prayer that morning! He had no thought of coming to Torch to work when he made his offer, but wondered if he could do anything at his home as his diabetic condition was "unstable" and he frequently had to go to bed. We told him about our need for cassette copying. He said: "Well, I'll have a go! I'll try it for a week or two and see." Ralph was ideal for the job, but he did have many difficulties with his health. He became very friendly with Sylvia, who was our secretary at the time. Altogether Ralph settled into the family very well; his humour and radiant faith blessed us all. In 1976 he married Sylvia, and the Lord provided them with a home in Nottingham. Ralph still does some of the tape work there, and he and Sylvia also spend much of their time in deputation work and following-up contacts amongst the Fellowship Groups and amongst blind people in the Nottingham area. Their home is always open for any from Torch House who want a few days' break.

After Ralph left, the work in the recording room went on. It has run much more smoothly in recent months since we welcomed John Claridge to the staff. He came with considerable experience of the technical side of recording. He has studied the whole system, and experimented with tapes to find the best for our purpose. He is ready to troubleshoot any time a machine plays up. This makes the whole department work much more satisfactorily. Kay, his wife, has experience as a scriptwriter and broadcaster. They are a very helpful combination.

Everyone who has anything to do with recording machines knows how easily they can deteriorate. Machines are costly, and sometimes difficult to obtain. At one time we were in urgent need of a Ferrograph machine. The work was in danger of stopping unless we could get one. Our enquiries indicated that these machines were very scarce. Then we heard of one, a reconditioned exhibition model, which was for sale. However, several other folk wanted it too. There was the added difficulty that we hadn't any money available to buy it. When the firm phoned us up they said: "We will sell the Ferrograph to you because you pay your bills promptly." This was a challenge to our faith which we could only pass on to the Lord. As fresh as if it was the first time it ever happened, we experienced a miracle, for the money came, the bill was paid promptly, and we were able to continue production without any more set-backs.

Money does not always come in so quickly, however, and sometimes we have had to ask the Lord for great wisdom when ordering electronic equipment costing £1,000 or more. The delay from placing orders to receiving delivery sometimes stretches into many months so we have to prayerfully anticipate our needs and our resources. It can be quite frightening to order by faith! And we have to be very sure in our hearts that it is God's will and time for ordering. Yet He is very gentle and good to us. On the occasions when money has been short and our faith very small, He has given us such peace and assurance that He will provide as we have waited on Him. He uses these times of want to remind us that He is the Source of all our money. If we always had money whenever it was needed, there would be no element of faith, or of waiting on him in prayer, when His love and care become very precious to us all, and when the whole of the Family is drawn closer together as they pray for the need.

When the magazines have been recorded, the masters prepared and copied, they are sent out in special plastic bags to the readers. All that the blind people have to do when they have listened to the recording, is to turn over the addressed card in the pocket on the bag, and the return address is automatically displayed. If you look closely, however, you see that the return address is not Hallaton! We shall have to take a trip down to Surrey to see the next part of the process.

Priscilla used to be our secretary. She in fact organised the structure of the office system in the early days at Hurstpierpoint. Then she met Robert, who was partially-sighted and confined to a wheelchair with multiple sclerosis. They both fell in love and married, and live in a bungalow near Redhill. Outside the front door is a large box for Torch post. When the cassettes are returned by the readers they find their way to this box. Robert wheels his way to it, opens it and calls: "Good, there's some work to-day!" or, "Only a few to-day—I wish they would hurry up and send them back." Robert's job is to listen, as readers often record messages on the cassettes. Some of these are in appreciation of the cassettes, some are complaints, many are recordings by lonely folk who are glad to have someone to talk to. Robert deals with each one and has regular tape correspondence with some of the people. Priscilla makes efficient notes of any matters which should be referred to the office, such as changes of address or orders for literature. Then Robert erases the cassettes, rewinds them, and packs them away to be sent back to Torch House. Tape letters are very time-consuming and we are delighted to have Robert's help in this way.

There is more to tapes than at first meets the eye, and we haven't yet looked at the Cassette Library or the Talking Book Section. Here are many titles of well-known Christian books, together with many Scripture portions, all ready to be sent out to readers. Let us take a look at the way these books are prepared, by going into the other booths in the Tape Department where this work is done.

For years we were aware that most blind people would never be reached by braille or moon type, because only a minority read embossed literature. We had to do something for the rest, and that meant that we had to look into the possibility of producing Christian Talking Books, which could be played on the same type of machine as that issued by Welfare organisations. To start with, we ordered the smallest Talking Book machine available. After several years when still no machine was forthcoming, we began to worry the makers. It was like getting blood out of a stone! Eventually we did get a machine and two slave copiers. All went well for a short time, but the standard of reproduction was not good, and the machines kept breaking down. "You are expecting these machines to do too much" we were told. "With a thousand readers you need a larger multi-copier than this."

"How much would that cost?" we asked. "Oh, about £1,700."

New Talking Book readers were frequently being introduced to us, and blessing was being brought to so many who had never heard the Gospel before. However, the recordings were often muffled and far from easy to listen to. We felt that we must take a step of faith and order the larger machine. Since those days we have had to order another copying unit which is now working full-time in the Talking Book section. Thanks to John's careful nursing and maintenance, the Talking Books are now of a much better quality. We are so glad that the Lord sent John with his expertise to help us to solve some of the problems and technical difficulties which this department has had.

The original recordings for the Talking Book and Cassette Libraries are made by volunteers in their own homes. A good original recording is essential, as the final play-back speed of a

131

Talking Book machine is as slow as fifteen-sixteenths of an inch per second. Any variation of recording volume, or any other fault in the recording is accentuated at this lower speed. We have a number of good volunteer readers now with machines capable of making clear recordings. How exasperating it must be, however, when a volunteer is in full spate and the baby cries, or a plane thunders overhead, or a youth decides to crack the ear-drums of the neighbourhood by riding at speed on his motor-bike! It is even more annoying when you have been talking into the microphone for half an hour, to discover that the "record" button isn't on! In spite of all this, we have a small but enthusiastic group of people who have passed the voice and equipment tests. They are making good recordings of the books selected for the Cassette and Talking Book Libraries. John has organised a scheme by which the readers check their own work, and thus discover before too long if they are making some bad mistakes in the recordings. These people who read for us have been blessed by the Lord themselves as they have been recording the books. "This book has been such a blessing to me as I have read it on to tape. It was more apt than you could have known when you sent it to me", is quite a frequent comment. Some of these volunteer helpers are disabled. "I'm more than grateful to the Lord for giving me the opportunity of serving Him in this way", said one. So you see how God blesses, right from the first press of the recording button to the finished product which goes to a blind person.

But we must pass on. When the original recording is finished, it is checked and edited. Then announcements have to be added at the beginning and end of each track. On a Talking Book cassette the maximum length of one track is two hours. Now the recording, which at this stage is still on an open spool, is ready to be fast-copied, track by track on to the Talking Book cassette itself. Each cassette can take six tracks if fully used, so quite long books can be recorded on to one cassette. In a good week, four new titles can in this way be added to the Talking Book Library, unless a large number of damaged cassettes have to be attended to and re-recorded.

The process for preparing the small cassettes is very similar, only the length of play is 45 minutes for each of two tracks instead of two hours on each of six tracks.

So we come to the point where the cassettes are ready for the Tape Library. The Librarian will classify the tapes and put them in the right section on the shelves. Then these cassettes will be ready to send out to readers in exchange for books which they send back. If ever any of our staff in this department feel discouraged, they have only to peep into a file of letters which have been sent in by grateful readers. We receive many letters which give a glimpse of how much this service means to those who receive it. The work of exchanging cassettes has to be done very prayerfully, of course, for only God knows which book will bring the most help to the recipient. The Librarians have often been used by the Lord, almost without them being aware of it, to send just that right book to help someone in need.

But some of the "readers" of Talking Books know nothing whatever about the Family, as they cannot enjoy embossed magazines and often do not possess small cassette recorders. They are quite unaware of other facilities, such as holidays and Fellowship Group activities. Also, these people are deprived of access to Christian news and magazines. It was to meet this need that the Talking Book magazine, "Reflections" was started. However, this project is very time-consuming, and so the magazine is only issued occasionally. It is eagerly awaited by Talking Book readers.

Some of the "Family" at Torch House help with small jobs in the recording studios, winding back the returned cassettes, or erasing some which need to be re-recorded. The whole department can at times give the impression of a bee hive; it is all so busy. Sometimes Talking Books have to be checked, as faults are reported in them. One day, one of the girls who has helped in this way was on a deputation tour. "Would you like to visit a blind lady?" she was asked. "Sure" she replied. Together with her host she went to the house of the blind lady. She was very old, and greeted them with great joy. It was obvious that she loved the Lord but she could not get out to any Christian Fellowship. Her face lit up when the girl came in. "Oh, you'll never know what these Christian Talking Books mean to me" she said. "I *live* for the next one coming from the moment I post a book back to you. God bless you for thinking of us."

That staff member came away deeply moved. Her job is tedious and routine at times, but she saw it in a new light after that visit.

Two other staff members called in to see a man who had been persuaded to have Christian books, though not professing any commitment to Christ. What a sight! He was bed-ridden, flat on his back, and his room was a medley of hoists and gadgets to help his wife to cope with the nursing. Yet, in that stricken home, Christian literature had been doing its quiet work, and had brought the joy of the Lord to both that man and his wife.

The Tape Department is the one which reaches people at their time of greatest need, when blindness has just come upon them. Electronics have opened up a door of opportunity which is especially suitable for the blind. We face a challenge, for we know that there is a need for cassette and Talking Book Libraries in every Fellowship Group; there is need for teaching and Bible study material, as well as dramatised recordings and other cassettes which could be used to introduce people to the Lord Jesus Christ. These are targets which we feel we should aim for, ways in which we could reach other blind people not yet in touch with the Libraries. However, we are very grateful that there are hundreds of people who at the press of a button can hear, "Hello Torch Family!"

CHAPTER 17 — NETWORK OF LOVE

"I am sure the chap who invented these little beauties had no idea how much they would mean to people like us," said a blind man as he fixed a C60 cassette into his machine.

Nowadays, many hundreds of blind people have their own machines, and spend hours recording and playing-back, corresponding and listening to "letters"—all because of these "little beauties" which are the product of electronic advance.

When Robert Nobbs undertook to check the magazine cassettes returned from "readers", he had no idea with what he was getting involved. Many of these cassettes came back with a little message of appreciation recorded on the end of the tape, but some had long outbursts of heart-felt feelings which showed the loneliness of the "readers". Other "readers" seemed determined to use up every bit of unrecorded tape, so they chatted for what seemed ages, probably making the real point they wanted to communicate in the very last inch of tape! Robert has taken up the challenge of this ministry, and listens patiently to each one, praying for the sender as he listens. Some of these "readers" obviously need to have more regular contact with us than magazines every month, and so there has grown up a network of people receiving and sending cassette letters. Robert himself corresponds with two or three men, but with all the checking and re-winding of tapes, he cannot tackle more. It was a great relief to Robert when Ralph Law offered to help him.

Ralph has a lively correspondence network himself now,

and feels he is getting to know the folk who "write" to him. He finds this means of communication very time-consuming however. One day he thought he would try an experiment. A man who corresponded with him seemed to feel he must fill the whole of a C90 cassette with his reply, so Ralph thought the man might be quite happy if a C60 cassette was used instead. The cassette came back, the C60 was filled—and another C60 was sent as well, also filled! Instead of listening for one and a half hours, Ralph had two hours' worth to listen to! Some of these people have nothing else to do all day.

As Ralph is himself diabetic, he has a special link with other diabetic people. Some of them are sorely tried by their illness. One man went for training to a Guidedog Centre. Whilst there, a serious condition developed in his legs. The doctor diagnosed gangrene, and said that the legs would have to be removed. Through the cassette network, the man asked for prayer for healing. Many people prayed; we prayed too in Chapel at Torch House; churches were asked to pray—and the legs healed. What is more, the man was able to have a guide-dog! His faith in the Lord began to grow from this experience. Now, he receives magazines and library books from Torch House, and is keen to play them over to his friends—"And all because, just at my lowest point, you sent me a tape, Ralph!" he said.

Another blind man heard about this experience and he became interested in linking up for prayer. He is a staunch Christian, and spends hours in prayer for people in need. Ralph keeps him informed of any special needs. "Don't tell me the details, just the names, and if they are Christians or not, and I'll take them to the Lord—He knows the details, that's all that matters!" he said.

Sometimes Ralph has to send tapes to folk who have lost loved ones—a wife or a child. What better than to pass on the wonderful words of Scripture to such people. At other times Ralph has to conduct a Bible study on cassette. "I don't see that it was necessary for Jesus to die—it was all a brutal mistake", or, "How can the Lord's prayer say 'Lead us not into temptation'?—surely God wouldn't tempt people!"

Ralph was glad to have the help and backing of his church, and his wife Sylvia too, so that a clear and correct answer could be given to such questions.

Ralph finds himself corresponding with all types, sufferers from terminal illnesses, and people of other cults and cultures. He has recorded his testimony, a glowing account of his experience of the Lord, as he has trod the pathway of suffering himself. We know that Ralph's cheery voice is a blessing to all those who listen. How he finds the time, with all his other Torch work, we do not know.

So many people wanted to be included in the network that, eventually, we had to set aside Marjorie Mason to tackle the job full-time. Working from her flat in Market Harborough, Marjorie corresponds with an ever-growing number of people. As she sends out her tapes, she comes across some who are strong in the faith, so she links them on with others who need to be encouraged and taught. This has formed a 'network of love' indeed, as the strong help the weak, and use their long hours of loneliness to real purpose.

Jean Spurgeon is one. She is bed-ridden and has very crippled hands, yet she is able to operate a cassette recorder. She spends time listening to the worries of others, and can point them to her Saviour in a way which the hale and hearty could not do.

One friend did not know that she had been sent a cassette letter; she thought it was a library book. She put it in her machine, and jumped when she heard, "Hello Alice!" For a minute she thought someone had come into the room! It was an absolute thrill to her to be able to hear a personal letter and not to have to get someone to read it to her. Now she has found joy in serving the Lord by helping in the 'network of love'. "I still tend to think you are with me in the room, Marjorie," she said. "The other day you had hiccups, and I nearly went to get you a drink of water!"

"I can tell you things on tape that perhaps I can tell no-one else," said one lady who was depressed to the point of being suicidal. Marjorie records extracts from poems, from books, from Chapel time at Torch, using the Choir, and houseparties—anything she can which will cheer the lonely folk, and help them to be part of the Family. That depressed lady has been so blessed that she is now corresponding with someone else who is suffering as she used to do.

Whenever possible, Marjorie links such people up with a live church or with a Torch Fellowship Group, for even this tape ministry is no substitute for face-to-face fellowship with other Christians. Marjorie finds a ready response from the Fellowship Groups, but she doesn't always manage so well when contacting churches, as they seem to be so busy!

And how this link is valued! "I can tell you, these tapes are a wonderful joy to me. They have often reached me just at the time when I needed them most. I want to praise the Lord for all the contacts I've made with the Torch Family, because He knows that I have adopted the Torch Family as my family, for they care for me more than my own family," was one sad remark.

Marjorie is a nurse, and often finds herself passing on a practical word of advice to someone who is suffering physically. She is glad to be of all-round service to her correspondents for Christ's sake.

I have known Marjorie to receive a distressing letter, drop all her plans for the day, and answer that letter straight away, so that it could catch the post. This happened once in the nick of time and saved a blind lady from making the mistake of linking up with some persistent Jehovah's Witnesses.

A lady who was "difficult" because underneath she was afraid, was also helped tremendously. She started to have Christian books, and changed from a position of hatred of God to one of trust before, at the age of ninety-two, she went to be with Him.

At times, Marjorie feels she must share the lovely world of nature with her cassette family. She even packed up some violets in polythene and sent them to one very lonely lady who couldn't sleep. She shares her holiday experiences too. Birdsongs, the cries of the gulls on the cliff-top, a description of the villages which she passes through, all bring a new dimension to the hearers. She recorded the sound of walking on the beach, and the waves of the sea as she paddled whilst on holiday. It was so realistic to one couple who were listening that the wife said, "Jim, you'd better roll your trousers up or they'll get wet!"

Sad to say, there are occasions when this type of ministry can be abused. Some people who are very sick in mind might invent problems for the sake of having attention. Marjorie has known a little of this too, and it would be wrong to give the impression that everyone to whom she writes is a "success story". When she finds out that people are abusing this particular service, she realises how needy they are—it is a call to prayer. However, such people are very few.

Cassettes certainly are tools of love in the hands of dedicated lovers of the Lord, but they can be used to spread gossip and harmful negative attitudes. This is why Robert, Ralph and Marjorie are most careful to link new people with those whose faith and outlook is wholesome and positive, and centred on the Lord Jesus Christ. They all realise how much they need the prayers of God's children in this ministry.

There is another cassette ministry which is proving very useful for those who are studying, or those who find they need to have access to material which is not available in braille. Frank Meech has undertaken to read any Christian literature, within reason, that is fundamental to the Word of God, and record it on to cassette. Since he started, he has been kept busy reading missionary magazines, study material, newsletters, and even whole study books, to the great delight of some of the studious members of the Torch Family.

So you can understand why it is that our blind friends are most grateful to the "chap who invented those 'little beauties'", for they have widened the horizons of many who have problems with their sight. In fact, they have introduced many to the Lord Jesus Christ, and to the 'network of love', which is His church.

CHAPTER 18 — "OH, I CAN READ IT!"

We had been speaking to a group of women at an afternoon fellowship. They had listened intently; in fact there had been a ripple of extra interest at one point. Now the meeting was over and I was trying to think what it might have been that had triggered off that extra spark of interest, when the leader came to me and said: "Would you come and meet Mrs. L? She is now registered blind and it has been a big shock to her." We sat down beside Mrs. L. and introduced ourselves. "I haven't been able to see print for six years," she said with a sigh. "I do miss my reading—I was such a bookworm and oh, I can't tell you how I miss reading my Bible." Mrs. L. seemed to have a certain amount of sight left, so I picked out a Gospel of Mark in quarter-inch bold capital letters, and handed it to her. She felt the outer blue cover, and opened it, shrugging her shoulders as if preparing for another disappointment. "Oh, oh!" she exclaimed. "I can read it, I can read it!" Tears streamed down her face as she proudly showed the Gospel to her friends.

We have been privileged to see such a scene many times as people have found that they could read our large print literature. There is a big gap between the 'eighteen-point' large print books which are to be found in most libraries, and the large print which we supply. The dividing line between poor sight and blindness is very varied, and in that "no-man's" land many people are groping about, straining to read newspaper headlines because they frantically want to keep up their reading. "Even your spelling goes to pieces when you can't see to read" one of them said.

Many people with failing sight are groping about for other reasons too. Some of them are deserted by their partners who cannot face living with the problems of blindness. This is a terrible blow, coming at the time when they most need help and encouragement. Some visually handicapped folk find the personal adjustments which are necessary too much, so they give up. Their houses and their clothes become dirty, and their one wish is to die. Others put up a brave fight and win through to success, finding ingenious ways of managing to do things by touch. But we have discovered many outwardly successful people who are puzzled, rebellious or sick at heart. They need something more than newspaper headlines to feed their minds. They need Christ!

We visited a club for the partially-sighted one day to talk about the work, and gave an invitation to any who were interested in Christian literature to step forward and examine the samples we had brought. The people came in a rush, eager to get something to bridge the literature gap, and to feed their minds. One young fellow of twenty-one strode off with a huge copy of St. Matthew's Gospel under his arm. "I'll show the fellows at work that I can read", he said.

At that same meeting a master from a school for the partially-sighted stood up and read a letter written by an eleven year-old boy. In it the lad thanked us for the magazines which came to his school. "Thank you so much, we love them. It is very good of you to send them to us for nothing!"

There are a number of schools for partially-sighted children in Britain, where there are young folk eager to have reading material. What an opportunity this is to pass on to them magazines such as "Spark" and "Flash" in large print.

Apart from the children's magazines, we issue "Torch" in large print, and also the magazine for the deaf-blind, "Our Mag". Many people registered deaf-blind have a little sight. Reading material is very important to them.

Our Large Print Library works on a postal lending basis similar to that of the Talking Books. We get a similar reaction from large print readers as we do from those who listen to

Talking Books. They are overjoyed to have missionary stories and devotional books to read, even if they have to read them with their noses to the page. The first large print hymn book which we printed was almost too popular. We charged a nominal 15p for it, selling it mainly to Fellowship Groups. The cost of producing it even then was nearer 50p. But old people's clubs and other groups got to know of it. We had to supply books to them at a more realistic price as unfortunately it would have made inroads on our resources. There is certainly a need for large print of this particular type.

The first thing we discovered when embarking on the production of large print was that we needed paper—lots of it! And as at that time we used duplicating methods of production, we couldn't use cheap paper either, as it would show the heavy black print through to the other side of the page, and spoil the sharp contrast between black and white which was so essential.

Just as we were getting into the full swing of production we had to face a paper shortage! "Paper?" our suppliers said. "Sorry, we can't send you any this month; there's a shortage you know." At Chapel time that day we were asked to pray about the problem. Next day we had a phone call from someone else: "Could you make use of an odd lot of top-quality duplicating paper?" "Could we WHAT?" And so the production line was kept in operation.

The method which we devised and used successfully for six years or more, was basically that of reproducing with an ordinary office duplicator. Originals were written by hand, by a team of experts, and an electronic stencil-cutter was used to prepare a stencil for each page. There were drawbacks. The stencils could be used quite a number of times, but in the case of Bible volumes they reached their limit and had to be renewed. It was essential to use thick duplicating paper, and the final product was very big and cumbersome as a result. But it worked, and it brought joy and the news of the Gospel to many people. However, particularly when it came to the Scriptures, hymn books and more regular booklets, it was not the ideal method.

Then Mr.& Mrs. Ballantyne, David's parents, retired and moved to the district. Jack, as he asked to be called, had been a master-printer and Florrie had helped him with binding and collating. They offered their services and their advice. It was such a relief to have someone who really knew what to do. Jack saw the possibility of using Off-set printing for Bible and book production. This would mean that thinner paper could be used and books could have a more lasting binding. It took some time to work out how much Off-set machinery we should buy, but the matter was settled when two machines were given to us. Then plate-making equipment was needed, and eventually a special typewriter to type some of the scripts for the print magazines, which could also be produced by the same process.

Meanwhile, we were nursing the dear old duplicator as it churned out its third time round the clock—millions of pages had passed through it! And the stencil cutter, long past its registered life, ground round and round—the wheels being kept going by prayer, of that we are sure!

Eventually, we were able to have two Off-set printing machines, and equipment for two types of plate-making. The difference was seen immediately!

Florrie was adept at collating—putting the books together from the piles of printed papers. It made our blundering efforts look so amateur and speeded up the large print production considerably. However, Jack and Florrie had come to the Midlands to retire, and here they were working harder than they should. We prayed for years, "Please send us an Off-set printer, Lord, so that your Word can really go out to the partially-sighted." No-one came. We had to wait several years, during which time John Oldham had become quite an expert on the Off-set machine, before others came to stand by John and help with braille and large print production. We do not know why we had to wait so long, but the new staff were well worth waiting for.

So the large print passes through the production line, and the booklets find their way to some surprising places. Prison, for instance! A testimony book was sent to a partially-sighted prisoner who had come to know the Lord. He was challenged about witnessing to the other prisoners. Eventually, that large print book went all round the prison, giving clear testimony to the saving power of the Lord Jesus. You never know where a bit of printed paper will travel!

The printed message can bring comfort to those who suffer and are in hospital. A lady was lying in bed, plunged into the depths of despair by a stroke. This had made her immobile, deaf and unable to speak and her sight was very dim. All she could do was weep and weep and weep! But she had a Christian nurse who sat beside her and tried to bring her the comfort of the Name of Jesus. Suddenly, the nurse had an idea. She managed to get hold of one of our large print hymn books, found the well-loved hymn, "The Lord's my shepherd" and pointed it out to the patient. The stricken woman nodded her head. Yes, she could read the print. Two verses of the hymn were on the one page, the other three were overleaf. Was the lady reading? At first the nurse wondered if she was. Then, in a few minutes, she signalled for the page to be turned over, so that she could finish the hymn. Yes, she was reading the message of that hymn. Soon she stopped weeping and was able to be comforted. The nurse was able to communicate with the woman from that point on. Praise God for large print! It may be bulky and expensive to produce, yet it is reaching people who need the comfort, and most of all, the Message of the Gospel.

One day a visitor to Torch House came into Chapel to join us in our two o'clock worship time. There she saw a girl, nose-to-page singing heartily from a large print hymn book. She felt challenged. At the flick of an eye she could read any hymn she wanted, and any book or magazine which took her fancy. She had often sung mechanically, without thinking of what she was singing. She thought of the times when she had read the Scriptures carelessly instead of listening to what they had to say to her. The sight of that girl struggling to read, reminded her of her privileges as a fully-sighted person, and she resolved to have a more responsible attitude to print in future.

Indeed, from those who have much shall much be expected!

CHAPTER NINETEEN — DOTS, DOTS, DOTS

Tony scratched his head. He had been doing that a lot since he began to think about moving the braille production department up to Hallaton. "You'll need several thousand cubic feet of space to take it all" he said. "There's storage of the finished booklets, storage of paper, storage of plates and room for the machinery too. You'll *never* find that amount; we'll have to build; it's expensive and it takes time. And what shall we do about production in the meantime?" As we faced this phase of the move in 1975, problems like this seemed insurmountable.

Tony went up to Hallaton to look more closely at the coach houses which we had earmarked for production. He measured them carefully. When he came back his face was a picture! "Do you know," he said, "those coachhouses are *exactly* the size I was asking for!"

There were repairs necessary before the production department could move up, but they were quite quickly effected and soon the rooms were ready to be put into use. As Tony had envisaged, they were the right shape to provide sections giving continuity to our production processes, and ending with a store for the finished articles. But this was a vast open space: "We'll need an awful lot of heavy shelving for this," Tony said.

Then we heard of an auction to be held in a bankrupt factory. Tony went. Later in the day two large lorries drove up to Hallaton, loaded with metal shelving. We stared in amazement. "I got it all for six pounds," Tony said. "Nobody wanted it. It cost us a bit to transport it, but I reckon we've got a good £600 worth of shelving there!"

Prisoners voluntarily spent their Saturdays for the next three months putting the shelves up. The shelving was just right for the job.

* * * * * * *

We must start much earlier though, if we are to appreciate the chain of miracles which brought this department into being. For years we embossed double zinc plates on a special electric machine, and transferred the dots to paper by using a wringer as a press. This method was back-aching and slow; we could seldom do more than 200 sheets in an hour and creases would form at the bottom of the page when embossing large-size sheets, which made the braille difficult to read. A number of other ideas were suggested for pressing but none of them survived the test—they just didn't work! Then we had a cheque for £2,000 earmarked "For your press". We had no knowledge of the donor! We started to look around, and examined a rotary press which we saw in use in Sweden, and which looked very good. We were told that it was made in Germany, and so decided to go to see it for ourselves.

February 1972 was very stormy, but we were not deterred as we booked our channel crossing from Dover to Ostend. We planned to go to Frankfurt and stay with our friend, Manfried, then go to Marburg to see the rotary press, with a view to ordering it. We estimated that the machine would cost nearly £4,000, allowing for transport. At the back of our minds we had an interest in a new electronic embossing machine which was made by the same firm, and which we would very much have liked. Ah well, we decided, we must concentrate on one thing at a time. But £4,000? We had only got £2,000—we could hardly go shopping for extras!

Next day, after our tickets had been bought, we had a phone call from a friend: "Just to let you know that I've put a cheque in the post from an anonymous friend, for £2,000!" £2,000 +£2,000=£4,000! What a great praise time we had in chapel that day!

The chain of miracles didn't end there. We crossed the Channel in a gale and were welcomed warmly in Frankfurt by Manfried and Elsa. We even managed to have a quick look round Saxenhausen, and sampled some of the famous sausages! Manfried kindly accompanied us on our trip to Marburg to interpret for us, as our German is non-existent. We arrived on the factory floor to see the rotary press being attacked vigorously by two muscular German workmen who were hammering and pushing with all their strength.

"What are they doing?" we asked.

"Oh, just changing a plate; it won't take long."

We thought of the blind boy we had hoped would operate the press. If this was how plates were changed, then he would never cope!

"You want it to be operated by a blind person? That is impossible!" they said.

Blank with disappointment, we stood on that factory floor, and sent up a quick prayer. Had it all been a mistake? Had we come all this way to see a machine that was no good? Something caused us to turn, and there in the corner, was a Heidelberg press adapted for printing braille, with a young girl operating it. The paper was being fed in automatically, and the "jaws" of the machine were well-protected.

"What about that?" we asked.

"Yes," they said. "It does good braille."

"Ah," we countered, remembering some of the unsuccessful research of the past, "but how do you get the two halves of the plate to stay in position? The braille would be ruined if there was any movement. Some braille printers have spent thousands of pounds trying to keep the plates in place."

"Oh, no trouble at all", the manager said. "We use double-sided sellotape!"

Incredulously we watched as he showed this simple method of positioning and holding the plates.

We bought a second-hand Heidelberg press in London, made the simple adaptations and—with the aid of double-sided sellotape—we were soon producing up to 2,500 sheets of beautiful braille an hour.

We had a look at the electronic plater whilst we were in Germany and brought home a sheaf of German notes to be interpreted. Later, we were able to buy the electronic plater as well as the Heidelberg Press for just £4,000! God's finances are very accurate!

If you go to the production block now, you will see two platers embossing braille in the first section. There, surrounded by curtains to absorb the sound, Carol Barnes is operating the electric plater. She is fully engaged on our English braille programme. She may have a 'dictator' sitting beside her, reading from print, or she may be copying from a braille 'original'.

On the opposite side of the room is the German electronic plater. This machine is used mainly for foreign braille. As we do not know all the languages which we emboss, nor their braille codes, we have to rely on braille 'originals' supplied by those who have this knowledge. Foreign braille can be printed by a blind operator on the electronic machine, as the braille characters of the 'original' can be felt with the left hand, and the machine operated with the right hand. If you know something about these things, you might ask, "But I thought two hands were required to print braille. How can you print a full cell of six dots when you have only five fingers?" This machine is so arranged that we can, in fact, operate six keys at once by using five fingers and the ball of the hand. There is a control for back-spacing, line-spacing and an automatic return when a line is completed. The machine can be operated with both hands if preferred. Its adaptability has made it useful for our foreign braille programme.

In the next section of the building, we see the Heidelberg press itself. We have fitted an extra large safety board so that the operator knows without a doubt when his machine is working. The press produces good braille which is easy and clear to read.

From the press the precious pages of dots go to the collating room where a honeycomb of partitions occupies most of the wallspace. A pile of 'page 1' is put in one pigeonhole, a pile of 'page 3' in another, and so on until the whole magazine is in order, and ready to be put together. Some of the Family come in and help to do this routine job. The checking is particularly wearisome, yet it is essential, and makes sure the job is well done. We have been very blessed with groups who come regularly from churches to help us with extra-large assignments. Girl Guides and school parties come too from time to time.

The next stage is the binding. Small magazines and booklets are stapled, and larger productions are punched and bound with plastic spines.

Lastly we come to the store. Books do not stay on these shelves for long. You will see the sacks of out-going mail stacked up near the far door. These may be going to many different countries; Hindi and Tamil to India; Hausa, Bemba and Swahili to Africa as well as many parcels of English braille, all go out from this department.

The quality of braille production depends a lot on the braillists involved. Carol is exceptionally good at English braille, but even so she is aware that mistakes can creep in. Every item needs to be proof-read. It is very difficult to find good proof-readers as this requires a high standard of braille. The foreign work needs to be proof-read thoroughly too. We are always looking out for careful proof-readers.

When mistakes occur, they have to be hammered out—resulting in a tell-tale 'tap-tap-tap' which sounds like a giant woodpecker. You can't keep quiet about your mistakes here!

We leave 'Production' to the clatter of Carol's machine and the voice of the person reading to her—they are brailling 'Flash': "quotes, if you follow Me, comma, you won't be stumbling through the darkness, comma, for living light will flood your path, stop, quotes, reference John Chapter 8 verse 12, end quotes".

And that is what the dots are saying to the fingers of blind people all over the world—people like Walter—he was arrested in his mad rush away from God, by a broken leg. As he was recuperating, the Lord met with him. He was born again. It was a healthy 'birth' too, for Walter found he had an insatiable appetite for Christian literature. He hung around Christian bookshops, and even bought print books, but couldn't read them as his sight was going. He persevered, and learned braille remarkably quickly. Again he frequented bookshops and Christian literature centres, searching for Christian braille. But no-one could help him. Poor Walter! He was crestfallen.

Then he attended the Keswick Covention, hungry for all the teaching he could get.

" 'Keswick Praise' is available in braille. Come to the front of the platform after the meeting if you are interested."

Immediately the last "Amen" had sounded, Walter rushed to the front, and bought the 3 volumes of 'Keswick Praise' in braille.

Back home, he began to think. Perhaps these people who printed the hymn book might have something else in braille. Walter wrote to us, and we supplied him with library books, magazines and tapes.

Later, at the Filey Crusade, he sought us out to tell us what a blessing these had been to him.

"I don't suppose you've got any new books for me?" he said, wistfully.

"Why, yes" we said, and began to pile new titles into his arms. His face was a picture of joy and satisfaction.

"But I've got a problem," he said. "I can't carry all these home, yet I want them—all of them!"

We arranged to send them to him by post when we got back home, thanks to the free post available for braille.

"Don't forget to send them" he said. "You don't know what these books mean to me."

We thought of the hours of planning, writing, brailling, checking, printing and despatching—"A word from a fellow like that confirms that it's worthwhile", we said, and thanked God for the encouragement.

CHAPTER 20 — BEHIND THE LINES

Some friends had called to see us, and as they had never been to Hallaton before they were full of questions.

"Can we have a closer look at the braille library?" they asked.

We walked through the winter garden which was a blaze of colour—blue plumbago flowers hung like a shower, red and salmon geraniums vied with passion flowers and rock plants. We came to the door marked "Library". At first the room looked dark and dreary after the beauty of the winter garden outside. Rows of braille books were stacked on the shelves from floor to ceiling. There were no eye-catching paperbacks here, just stiff dark covers and brown manilla paper. The only touch of colour was found on the spines of the volumes, maroon for study books, yellow or gold for devotional, green for missionary, and a few blue spines here and there.

Yet, in spite of the dull appearance of this library, I doubt if any books are more cherished and laboured over. For the contents of this room are appreciated all over the world.

But to understand their worth, it is necessary to look behind the lines of braille dots, and to see all that is involved in putting a title on the shelves.

These books have titles which are well-known in most Christian bookshops, and which might be seen on many a church bookstall. But the way they are changed from compact print to these bulky volumes is a story of great sacrifice and perseverance.

154

The first stage in the transition is the Book Committee, an all-day marathon which is usually held once a year to select books suitable for transcribing. Serving on the Book Committe is a group of people who have special skills, and a knowledge of the needs of blind people. Two workers from the Christian Literature Crusade bookshop bring over two hundred books to be considered. Rosemary Adams, whose husband is on our Central Committee, works at the local C.L.C. bookshop so she has been busy for the past year, investigating new titles as they are published. Books which might be suitable are read and commented on by different individuals, who write out their comments. Rosemary files these to produce at the actual Book Committee, when the decision has to be made whether to pass the book for brailling or not. In this way a fair assessment of each title can be made.

We sit round the table—librarians, editorial staff, field workers, teachers, all with particular needs in mind.

"This is a gentle story. It would be suitable for some of Marjorie's elderly contacts", says one.

"I hope we can have a few meaty study books this time", says one of our more studious members.

"Well," says our chief librarian, "I hope they won't have too many footnotes. I can spend as long as five hours deciding if they should be incorporated in the text, or listed at the end of the volume. You can't have footnotes at the bottom of the page in braille!"

"I thought this book 'waffled' too much" says another. "It has taken the author three pages to start! That means it will run into four or five volumes in braille; it will give the transcriber a lot of unnecessary hard work."

"Yes," says one of the field workers. "That sort of book discourages the slower readers, and they need all the encouragement we can give them. I wish some of the writers would know what they wanted to say, and then say it in a straightforward way."

The representative from the bookshop dives into his box of books. "This is very good" he says. "It is brief, but scriptural, and it covers some interesting points adequately." Heads nod. Others on the Committee have enjoyed that book.

Of course, brevity is not the only standard by which a book is judged suitable. Longer classics, books by C. H. Spurgeon, or Dr. Martyn Lloyd-Jones, or F. B. Meyer are very much sought after by the more fluent readers. Tozer is another favourite, and missionary stories, biographies and travel books are very popular. Some books are never out-of-date. "By Searching" is still bringing great blessing and challenge to readers. Recent accounts of world-wide missions are needed too, and books which deal with problems of marriage and racial matters.

The books chosen are stacked on the table ready to be listed so that we can pay the shop for them. This year a Sunday School is collecting money to help pay for these books!

The next step is to procure copyright, without which no book can be put into braille, large print, or on to tape. This job falls to the lot of Rosemary Adams. She carefully lists the titles under the heading of the different publishers. The copyright holders may not always be the publishers, and have to be traced through them. Rosemary must carefully note whether we require the book to be brailled for one single copy or produced for bulk distribution, written in large print, or recorded. From her list, Rosemary begins her task of writing to the publishers. Some publishing houses are most helpful. They understand what we are doing, and give us all the assistance they can. Many of them will not even charge a fee. Sometimes a letter is returned, as the publisher has gone out of business. At other times we can only get copyright permission in part, and must write to another publisher for clearance. Sometimes three or four letters have to be written to obtain copyright for one book.

"We have given permission for this book to be brailled by an American agency", wrote one American publishing house, "so we do not think it necessary to give it to you." Another letter: "We want to put it in *English* braille. The American braille system is not quite the same as ours." Yet another letter: "What is the difference?" "Well, the braille contractions are different—and anyhow, such a popular book as this is needed on library shelves here in Britain." Final letter: "O.K. Permission given!"

Then, of course, each firm has its own requirements as to how we acknowledge the copyright in the front of the finished book. The wording has to be exact whether written or recorded. Conditions for copyright are quite stringent these days, and become even more exacting each year. This is especially true for recordings, which could be a threat to sales. In our experience, the opposite is the case. Listeners write, "This wonderful book has been such a blessing to me that I would like to buy several print copies to distribute among my friends." — "I have told the young people at my church about this title, and urged them to buy a copy." The publishers get quite a bit of free publicity when they give us permission to reproduce their titles.

Rosemary does have some interesting insights into the ways of publishers. She wrote to a publisher in the U.S.A. for permission to copy a certain book in braille, large print and on talking book. The firm replied asking, "How many copies?" (We had mentioned one in braille, one in large print and probably a dozen on Talking Books.) They granted us permission eventually, but sent a form asking for yearly reports on who borrowed the books, and how often. Our librarians nearly fainted! And after all that, the book was not particularly suitable.

But Rosemary has other, happier memories of her copyright experiences. We asked a missionary in Brazil for permission to braille his book for our library. When replying, he sent us his prayer letter, which was very interesting. We sent him a copy of "The Torch Family". Later on we were most surprised and touched to receive a cheque from him.

The obtaining of copyright permission is only the first hurdle to be overcome "behind the lines"! The next step is to send the print book to a transcriber. We try to match the titles to the transcribers as far as possible, as it makes the task more pleasant if the worker enjoys the book. This is important when you think that to produce one copy of a book in braille can take a year or more, as some of the books run into eight or nine volumes.

How do people come to offer their services as voluntary braille transcribers? "I heard of the need in a meeting, and felt urged to help", said one. "I had a problem, because I had such irregular hours of work that I could not do the usual type of Christian service. Transcribing is the answer for me." A young mother said "I can do transcribing in my own home, when I am alone at nights and the children are in bed." One lady was vaguely interested in learning braille, but had never 'got around' to approaching us to have details of our postal instruction course. She was at a Ladies Conference at which I was the speaker. However, just after the start of the meeting, as I had started to speak, she was taken ill and had to rush out. On her way out she took a copy of the braille alphabet from the table. "If I can learn this in two days, then I'll apply to take the transcribers' course", she said. She was in bed for the rest of the conference, but she did manage to learn the alphabet. She kept her promise, and became a valued member of our transcribing team.

What are the qualities which make a good braille transcriber? Anyone who is careless and untidy by nature is probably not suitable. A person who is really bad at spelling would be unwise to transcribe. People who are always feeling under pressure, "terribly busy", or who are not able to organise their leisure, or who like to hop from one job to another are likely to "fall by the wayside." A good transcriber is consistent, careful, disciplined and even maybe pernickety over details. Reasonable intelligence is needed to learn braille and apply it, and it helps to have a fairly good memory, though at times, even when taking the transcribers' test, it is permissible to refer to the primer. It is not necessary to be quick, but it is essential to be accurate. Transcribing admirably suits the perfectionist!

Before a would-be transcriber can start to do the postal insruction course, it is necessary for him to have a brailling machine. In our experience the best braille for library use, with all the journeyings to and fro which the books have to make, is produced by the Stainsby braille writer. These machines can be bought at concession price by any who are seriously considering taking the course or, when we have spare machines available, we can lend these to beginners who are not quite sure if they will be able to complete the course.

Transcribing can be a lonely business, as it lacks the stimulus attached to church work. Yet we are again and again made aware of how valuable this work is. We have seen outlooks change as blind people are introduced to Christian literature.

There are other difficulties for transcribers to face. "I had a complaint from the lady in the flat below mine", wrote one of our helpers. "She couldn't understand what it was that was causing a certain 'thump, thump' which she heard every evening!" We suggested that a foam-rubber mat placed under the brailling machine might eliminate the problem with the neighbour. We were filled with admiration for another transcriber who had an incurable back condition which made it essential for her to lie flat on her back for a period each day. How could she use this time of enforced rest for the Lord? By sheer ingenuity and determination she propped the print book in front of her on a tilted bed-table, put the Stainsby machine on her body, and worked at her braille from a recumbent position. Her braille was good, too!

One transcriber moved to a new home in a small village. Soon word went round the village that she could "print braille". People began to call to see what she was doing, and she soon made friends with her new neighbours. Eventually, the vicar became interested in taking the course. He proved to be an excellent pupil, and passed the test in three months. It is helpful if transcribers can live near enough to encourage each other.

Transcribing is not a costly thing except in time and patience, so we were surprised to hear one transcriber complain that it was proving expensive. "Why is it expensive?" we asked. "You can get braille paper very reasonably as a voluntary worker, and we send you the book to be transcribed." "You don't understand," he said. "You see, by the time I have brailled the book, I feel I can't live without it, so I have to go to the bookshop and buy a copy for myself." He was one of our quickest transcribers so we understood.

"What would you say was the longest book you have brailled?" we were asked. I think the "New Testament Commentary" would be the longest. It ran into thirty-six braille volumes, and took a very active transcriber three years to complete! It is well used!

If you look closely at our library shelves you will see other books besides braille. The large print library has not so many titles as the braille section, because it has not been in existence so long, but it is very much appreciated. As in the braille library, these books are individual copies prepared by hand. The work of writing a book in large print requires a similar temperament to that of a good braillist, although there is no need to take a postal course to learn how to write. Practice and care over forming each letter are needed, and it can take at least half an hour to write one page of large print. We usually ask people to submit a page of capital lettering if they wish to help us in this department. In this way we can find out any irregularities of style, or any unusual curls or shapes which would make their work difficult for the reader. Usually, it is the person with neat, round, upright writing who makes the best Large Print writer. Some people have a style of writing which is difficult to adapt, although they have tried again and again to change it. One or two people have been so exasperated that they have told us we are fussy! But when they watch partially-sighted readers, nose to paper, trying to stand in the best light in order to read, they usually understand. Pens which 'fade' into grey are one of the problems of large print writing. The contrast of black and white is most important.

Large print books are quite easy to proof-read, but with braille, the system is more complicated. Here we rely on competent blind people to proof-read a transcriber's work, chapter by chapter, and to send it back to the transcriber complete with a list of mistakes. It is essential to re-write a page on which there is a mistake. Sometimes transcribers have squashed out a few dots, hoping they would stay down. Invariably they rise up again, and make nonsense of the text to a blind reader. Our chief librarian, Eileen Cole and her assistant, Margaret McKinstrie, are always on the look-out for 'rubbings out' before they send the sheets off to be bound, ready to put on the library shelves.

"Why do you have just one copy of a book? Why not get it produced in bulk?" is a question which many people ask. The answer lies in the fact that because braille is so bulky, most readers would have room for only a few titles in their homes. The King James version of the Bible has seventy-four volumes, for example, and needs a five-foot shelf. So it is general practice among braille readers to borrow most of their reading matter from a library. There are several good secular libraries and a library for students, but they do not cater for the spiritual needs of readers on the whole.

There are some books on the library shelves which are neither in braille nor large print. These are the Moon type books, which are embossed with a script which uses segments of the Roman Alphabet instead of dots. This type is easy to learn and to feel, so it has a use for those who go blind later in life. It is specially helpful for the deaf-blind, as they cannot gain any help from tapes. There are drawbacks with this type, however. It is very much more bulky than braille, and is not easy to produce. In fact, it is only printed in one place in the world, in Reigate, Surrey. So we have to rely on books chosen by the R.N.I.B. to fill our Moon section, and there are not many Christian books printed. Our main contribution to Moon readers is our magazine programme. However, here on our shelves, we have a few Christian books, which are very precious to the small number of people who read Moon type.

Every day the postman backs his van up to the library door. Out come five or six sacks full of library books to be changed. We are sometimes privileged to see blind people enjoying their library books, but more often we hear by letter what this service means to them.

"I am really improving with my reading. After I had read this wonderful book to myself, I read it to my friend. We just could not wait to read the next chapter—we were so enthralled", wrote one lady, who had lost her sight later in life.

"I am the type who is best helped by other people's experiences—where I can see some useful purpose in being 'laid aside'. I loathe inactivity." That came from a lady who had bitterly resented becoming deaf and blind. It was wonderful to see the change which came into her life as a direct result of her access to Christian reading. Her bitter attitude became sweet, and her life found new purpose. Many people have had this experience. It makes all the struggles and the hours of labour worthwhile to be able to help such people.

So you can see that a great deal of activity goes on 'behind the lines' to bring Christian literature within the reach of those questing fingers!

CHAPTER 21 — IF ALL WERE EASY

"If all were easy, if all were bright
Where would the Cross be, where would the fight?
But in the hard place, God gives to you
Chances of proving what He can do."

"I should think that everyone who comes to stay at Torch House becomes a Christian", said one of our friends, after spending a weekend with us.

But do they?

We can look back on a number of people with whom we seemed to have failed, people who have come in touch with Christ, but for one reason or another, have turned away from Him.

It was just like that when our Lord was on earth.

In the North aisle of Truro Cathedral there is a terracotta panel which shows the Lord Jesus on His way to His crucifixion. There, carved in stone, we have the reactions of people when faced with the Lord Himself—and there were many who would not have His offer of life. Pilate is shown standing there with a look of helplessness on his face. His wife, beside him, is a picture of despair. Simon of Cyrene, with rippling sinews, has his arm round the heavy log which will eventually be the upright post of the Cross. Barabbas stands, looking stunned at being free. Then there are the sad, weeping women of Jerusalem; the scornful, mocking faces of the Pharisees; the two condemned robbers, chained to Roman soldiers, one with shoulders set in stubborn determination, the other with a look of wistfulness and fear. The panel is a fine carving, and a real character-study, revealing just how differently these people were affected by the central Figure—The Lord of Life Himself.

As we look back we have, carved in our memories, the figures of some who have come to stay with us at Torch House, but who, when faced with the reality of the Presence of Christ, have turned away from Him. For, although many have come to know Him, and have been changed by His love, a few have reacted in unbelief or indifference. However, just as those characters carved on that beautiful panel in Truro Cathedral went on in history, some to find the Saviour, some to utterly reject Him, so as we look at our 'disappointments' we realise that the story in most cases is not complete—there is still hope that the message of the Cross will reach them.

Mr. A. came to Torch House for an Easter Houseparty. He was a very sensitive blind person. He loved music, especially organ music, and was a "good-living, church-going, model citizen". His faith was centred in the ritual and ordinances of his Anglo-Catholic church so much that if he had to choose at any time between what his church wanted and what the Lord wanted, he would choose to follow his church. It soon became apparent that he found the challenge of a houseparty too much! He felt ill at ease when we talked of loving the Lord, and he badly missed his organ music, especially as it was Eastertime. He found it hard to mix with the non-conformists who were in the majority at that houseparty. And, somehow, he felt uncomfortable when commitment to Christ was mentioned. He had put his faith in beautiful music, and here there was only spontaneous singing—to a piano at that! He loved the richness of tradition, the solemn chanting, and the beautiful words of the prayers with which he was familiar. Here, folk were talking their hearts out to God in everyday language. It made God seem so commonplace to Mr. A's reasoning. And so he missed the heart of the matter. He failed to have a personal encounter with Christ. He put up with the houseparty for a day, then, murmuring some polite excuses, he went home—empty.

We were faced with quite another problem when Mr. B.

came. He professed to be a true 'born-again' believer, and a voluntary colporteur at that. He had just a little sight, and he busied himself around the place, helping in many ways. But there was something odd about him. We didn't know what it was, but it gave us a vague uneasiness when he was with us. One night, in the early hours of the morning, one of our boys came rushing into the bedroom in great distress. Mr. B. had shown what it was that made him seem 'odd', for he was a homosexual. A week of great strain followed, as on one hand we felt the need to safeguard our young people, and on the other, to try to help this needy fellow. Dear Grandad was with us then and he spent many hours talking and praying with him. Eventually Mr. B. left, saying that he would keep in touch with us. He didn't come back, but later he wrote a most unpleasant note saying that he wanted no more of our . . . . literature. When things go wrong we are drawn to a new place of nearness to the Lord, but we cannot avoid the sorrow of seeing lives ruined by the enemy.

Mrs. C. came to us as a very last resort. She was blind, rather demanding, and alone in the world. Could we have her for a few weeks until more permanent accommodation could be found? We re-arranged bedrooms, and by asking folk to share, we managed to take her in temporarily. In her time she had been a beautiful actress. But now her lovely blue eyes were sightless, and her beauty had faded. She was old and very frightened.

"I'm terrified, my dear," she said, "just terrified!" Her voice rose in anguish. "I'm so afraid to meet my Maker!" We spent many hours with her, reading, talking and praying. She was unable to grasp the fact that the Sacrifice which the Lord Jesus Christ made on Calvary for our redemption was actually PLANNED in eternity past. "I think the Crucifixion was a ghastly mistake" she cried, "hounding a good man to a martyr's death!" The fact that the "martyr" was the Son of God Who, at any time could have escaped His captors but Who willingly gave Himself for our sakes, was too much for Mrs. C. to grasp. Her old brain could not take it in. She moved on, still terrified to die, and yet unable to understand the way of Salvation. She taught us the solemn fact, "My Spirit will not always strive with man"—there comes a time when it is too late to receive God's offer of mercy.

Mr. D. was a positive thinker, the sort of blind person who is continually trying to prove himself. He was doing well too, though perhaps success was developing a hardness in his character. He was very interested in radio and had prepared a number of programmes which had been accepted by local radio. He was now preparing others which would be specifically of interest to blind people, and he hoped to distribute these through the whole radio network.

He came to us for a day, interviewing the staff, recording the sounds, and generally documenting the work. The staff gave clear answers to his questions, and he seemed well pleased with his day's work. Finally he interviewed us. "Just in one sentence, Mr. Heath, what would you say to sum up the work you do here?" Dad Heath looked at the mike, and at the reels slowly turning on the Uher tape recorder. He isn't one to give quick one-sentence summaries! He replied after a pause, "We are sure that Jesus Christ is alive to-day for we have seen His Hand at work changing lives—this is what our work is all about. Jesus Christ will change anybody's life, including yours, if you let Him."

The confident look left Mr. D's face, and it crumpled in an attempt to restrain the tears. He swallowed hard. "I'm sorry," he gulped. "I'll record the end of the programme when I feel more composed. I'm evidently not as hard as I care to think I am."

We watched him as he trailed away with his tape recorder in his hand. What a help he could be in spreading the Gospel—if only he would yield to the Saviour!

Things can go wrong in other areas as well as with guests, areas which can hurt even more! Trusted friends on whom we have relied suddenly drop the friendship because of evil rumours being spread around. It hurts! Promising workers get diverted, or find the cost of discipleship too hard. They leave a gap which aches. Some folk of whom we have high hopes, find they cannot stand the pace, and they 'go under'. We suffer with them. We are often faced with our own mistakes too—our inadequacy, our unwise handling of a problem, our impatience with someone who disappoints us. People often quote Romans 8:28—so often that we tend not to listen—but it is true, gloriously true. Nothing, nothing at all comes the way of a believer by accident—it is all by design. Through all the trials, we are learning to be more like Christ. Our friends may fail, but then so do we. When Abraham failed, when David sinned, when Peter denied his Lord, did He forsake them? No! he went on trusting them and blessing them beyond all that they deserved. What grace! Our failings and the failings of others only make that grace seem the sweeter!

At times God uses the very disappointments of life to show us gaps in our programme, and areas where He wants us to advance.

We had a long-distance phone call from a young man who had just had a very unpleasant experience with a fortune-teller which he wanted to forget, but couldn't. He was very keen to know the truth about salvation. We talked on the phone, and wrote long letters to him in braille. We introduced him to Bible Studies and lent him Scripture portions. He lived in a remote country area where we had no Fellowship Groups, and where we knew of no Christians who lived within reach. He continued to keep in touch, working at his Bible study course, and phoning us frequently. Soon he professed conversion. One day he phoned excitedly, "Some folks have visited my home and have read to me from the Bible. They are going to take me to their church." Weeks passed and we heard no more. We wondered what had happened. Then he phoned, hard and curt. "I don't want any more of your literature. I'm a Jehovah's Witness, and I'll get all I want from them."

If only we had links in that area! If only there was a Fellowship Group within reach, or a Prayer Group to take that boy on their hearts. That disappointment prompted us to pray for the rural areas of our land, and was the beginning of our vision for "Torch Home Groups", which could be run with only two or three people, but which could provide folk such as this boy with love, care and fellowship.

There are other things which sometimes puzzle us, but which are part of those "all things". Some Christians have a strange philosophy concerning the blessing of the Lord, and interpret it as something purely material. The Lord had to deal with us on this one!

We had grown used to hearing people say, "Isn't it marvellous! These people just pray, and see, next day they have all that they need. It's just like George Müller all over again, or Hudson Taylor!" Even more subtle is the thought, "God always looks after His children; look at their cars and nice houses. He honours them with money, doesn't He!

So, creeping into our thinking was this idea that if Christians didn't prosper and have a high standard of living, they were not walking with God. It could easily grow into the theory that successful people are right, and others who have their share of poverty and trial are wrong.

Yet, we knew of those who were grieving the Lord and yet were materially prosperous, and of others whose lives were full of the beauty of Christ, and yet they were poor. It hurt even more when the Lord allowed our own "brook Cherith" to begin to dry up. At a time like this, the Psalmist went "into the sanctuary" and then he understood. So that is where we went!

There, in the secret place with God, we learned to have His view of our life, our work, our prosperity. And it was diametrically opposite to that of some of our Christian friends. God said, "Abraham, sacrifice your son"—so God proved him and prepared him for a deeper walk with Himself. The children of Israel, still flushed with the victory at the Red Sea were led, actually *led by the Pillar of Cloud* to Marah, where the water was too bitter to drink! Why? "There God proved them" to see if they would follow Him without question or complaining. They did not pass this test very well at all, but even so He led them on to the rest and shade of Elim.

We had a look at the New Testament, and saw Philip facing a great crowd who needed a meal. "Where shall we get bread?" asked the Lord. "This He said to prove him!" Philip started to do his sums, but Jesus swept them aside and showed His power in the face of an impossible situation. Provings are for a purpose. Tests reveal something more of the power and greatness of our God.

These thoughts were very much to the fore in our minds during the Summer of 1979. For months inflation had been pushing up prices. The oil crisis combined with the bad weather to make Winter 1978/1979 devastatingly expensive. Also we were committed to seeing the bathroom block completed—all out of current income. Christian giving seemed to be at a very low ebb, as many of our sister missions were discovering. Soon we found ourselves facing bills for commodities which were very necessary if we were to continue the work: £2,000 for talking book equipment which was desperately needed; £1,000 for cassettes; £2,000 for braille paper, apart from every-day living expenses. It became very meaningful when we prayed, "Give us this day our daily bread." Had God forgotten us? No! Never. Were we failing Him in some way? We had several sessions of prayer, opening our hearts to the Holy Spirit, but we found real peace and joy in His presence. Still the "skies were as brass", or rather, the income was low!

Some of our friends in other missions were fighting similar battles. Just a few felt they must "do a little sophisticated begging", and others decided to cut-back on their work. What could we do? It seemed that God was pointing to expansion. Large Print production, Tapes and Talking Books, foreign braille and the new course for young people, Christian Service Training, all demanded more money!

"He led them there to prove them, whether they would wholly follow His way or not."

We might not have noticed the sterling worth of our staff if this experience had not come our way. All who join us as staff do so ready to trust the Lord for all their needs. We always channelled 20% of our income to be used for staff, and as the actual amount of money we were receiving was about the same as before inflation, we were able to pay the staff their small allocation regularly, so they had been cushioned from the effects of the cost of living. Only those in charge of the buying were aware of the battle to have faith for the necessary supplies. But God wanted us all to share it. We talked it over. All, without exception, wanted nothing to do with fund-raising efforts of any sort. It was a great strength to us to see how the staff stood together in this. They even accepted a reduction in their meagre pocket money, and went without extras to help to ease the situation. So we stood together, just believing that God could and would supply our needs.

It was precious to us! There were the Unions driving with all their force to get pay of £100 a week for their members, and here were a handful of believers, willing to manage on far less than that a month for Christ's sake.

And we discovered we were in good company. In spite of the wonderful stories of provision which George Müller, Amy Carmichael, the Mary Sisters and others could tell, they also knew the experience of similar testings.

CHAPTER 22 — EVERYTHING TO GOD IN PRAYER

It was January 1974, and the staff were taking a weekend away from Torch House so that they could spend time in prayer and fellowship together. We had no special speaker, but shared devotions among ourselves. On the first night it was Rona's turn to give the epilogue. She was very nervous as she read in Mark 16 "He upbraided them for their unbelief." When she reached the verse, "These signs will accompany those who believe: in My Name they will cast out demons; they will speak in new tongues; they will pick up serpents, and if they drink any deadly thing, it will not hurt them: they will lay their hands on the sick, and they will recover", Rona broke down. "We are not showing any of these signs, none at all" she said.

Her obvious sincerity touched us all. Oh, we *were* having blessing if you looked at conversions and increased opportunities, but signs such as these—well, to be honest, we had never even wanted them.

Yet we were disturbed when we saw the way one or two of the young folk were struggling along. They were not at peace; they had very little joy. They seemed to have so many blocks, hang-ups and problems. We couldn't get to the bottom of it all. They had co-operated with us in every way they could with Bible reading, prayer, repentance, self sacrifice, witness, even feeble attempts to praise—but still they failed to rise from their depression. Was there a greater Power in Christ which we had not experienced as a Family, up to now?

It was houseparty time, and a crowd of visitors was gathered in the lounge, singing: "Christ is the answer to my every need". What a lot of needs were represented there! Blindness was by no means their only problem! Some of them needed to hear the message of salvation, others had never started to grow in Christ. There were a lot of 'chips on shoulders' in that room too! Did I really believe that Christ was the answer? Or was I merely singing it because it was something Evangelicals subscribed to?

"Oh Lord, make me real. Let me know Your Power in a new way. Prove to me that You are adequate for every need, I pray."

Some time later we had a visitor who had suffered from depression for four years. She had attempted suicide, and had been advised to attend a mental hospital but had run away.

She was sedated, and in poor shape physically, and was under the care of a psychiatrist. She came to us for a weekend, but spent most of the time hidden in her bedroom. She wouldn't even come out for meals—the atmosphere of the house upset her! The staff were so kind and loving, and talked to her as long as she would let them. Then suddenly she came out and asked to see us to talk over her problems. She had often talked to her psychiatrist, and found no relief. We were very doubtful if we could help her at all.

"Here we are again, Lord, another lot of need. Oh, please give us faith to claim the Power of Your Name, and to believe that You *are* the answer."

That girl talked as she had never talked before. She took several hours to tell out all the horrors of the past, and the problem relationships in her life. As she talked, we silently prayed, handing it all to the Lord. We didn't know what else to do!

Then we prayed with her. Bit by bit the Lord brought facets of her history before us, and we took them to Him together. It was as if He was sharing her shock, and soothing her fears. "I hate so-and-so, and I don't intend to speak to him again", she said at one point. We turned to the Scriptures to discover the way our Saviour would react to misunderstanding and abuse. As she knelt before the Cross, that girl found forgiveness and healing for all her festering sores. She went away completely changed.

What had we done? Just taken 'everything to God in prayer!' We began to realise that 'blanket' prayers were not effective in this sort of situation, for each detail had to be faced honestly and without exaggeration so that it could be touched by the power of the Cross, and in the authority of the Name of Jesus.

It was the beginning of a new step of victory! The Name of Jesus; "His Name, through faith in His Name, has made this man whole", said Peter in Acts chapter 3. Christ *was* the answer, it was just that we hadn't applied His Name and Authority in a spirit of believing prayer!

As we turned to help our own Family, we felt we had a new

strength, and a new concept of prayer. It wasn't new, of course. It was used repeatedly by the Apostles, and by discerning people throughout the history of the Church, but it was a new experience to us. We found it necessary to have absolute truthfulness one with another, and it was no use trying to help anyone unless our hearts were filled with pure love and tenderness for them. We found that the Lord poured this love into our hearts more and more as we asked Him. If this didn't happen, then the time of prayer was barren and powerless. Some of our young folk responded quickly to this type of believing prayer, but others had so much sorrow in their lives that we had to help them gradually. Healing of the mind, we discovered, always had to happen gently.

We had so much to learn, we still have, as these areas of mind and memory are like uncharted seas, but we are perfectly safe upon them if we keep to the principle of letting the Lord do the work. For this reason we do not ask questions or probe about to find out the sores in people's minds; we pray to the Lord to reveal them if He wants to do so. How comforting it is to let Him take control, as we take 'everything to God in prayer.'

"Do you know, Mum Heath," said one of the girls one day. "I think the Lord Jesus did something like this to Peter. You know, he denied the Lord three times. He must have had awful memories of that time, and so the Lord gave him the chance to say three times that he loved Him." "Yes," I said, "and isn't it interesting that both happenings were as Peter was beside a charcoal fire. I dare say that helped Peter to relive his failure and to make a new, honest start to his discipleship."

But, precious as this new believing prayer was, there were still problems that were not solved.

"Do you love me?—really?" I think this question came up twenty or more times every day from one of our folk. The insecurity and emotional upheaval of her childhood seemed to be taking a long time to heal.

"Please, please, oh *help* me" she said. "I *hate* always coming to you with this same silly question. My head knows that you love me, but I can't make my heart believe it, and I feel so bad!"

I felt bad too, because I couldn't think what else I could do. "Dear Lord, I can only claim the all-powerful Name of Jesus, when I ask You to help this girl. Heal her emotions, Lord, please."

As I bowed in prayer, a text sprang to my mind: "I will take the stony heart out of your flesh and will give you a heart of flesh." I didn't think it was relevant, so I brushed it aside, and continued in prayer.

"Oh dear. Oh, oh dear." The girl sat holding her heart and crying out "oh dear" for about ten minutes. What was happening? What had I done? Then a lovely rest and peace filled my heart. Of course, all I had done was to take 'everything', even this strange problem, 'to God in prayer.' No harm would come as a result of that—only good.

At length, the girl spoke. "Mum Heath, it was just as if God cut out a big stone from my heart. I feel different now. I can take it when you say you love me." I understood then why I had that text about the stony heart.

That girl, all through this time, had never doubted the love of God in Christ, but humans had so often hurt and forsaken her that she had become hard inside, so that she couldn't feel safe in trusting human love at all. She very seldom asked us if we loved her after that, and she began to love herself, too, which resulted in her going out in love to others. The process of healing in her emotions was slow, but it was sure, because God was the One Who was working in her.

We were just beginning to see 'signs following'.

Occasionally we have come across deeper problems still, where people have been afflicted by powers too strong for them. This was sometimes because, as children, they had been exposed to spiritualist healing by parents who were anxious to see their blind children healed. This exposure, in some cases, brought untold harm to the child, and only by claiming the power and authority of the Name of Jesus over the enemy, could the afflicted person be healed. However, we have seen some wonderful people emerge when they have been freed from this evil bondage.

Yet, we have never seen anyone healed of blindness! We have known some instances of physical healing, and mental and emotional renewal, but we have not even felt led to pray for healing from blindness yet. Strange as it may seem, not many of the younger blind people crave for the gift of sight.

One of our blind staff told us of an experience she had which shows this point. She was sitting in the front of a church during a healing meeting, when two people came to her, and said that they felt they should lay hands on her so that she could be healed. She was very surprised. "Healed?" she said. "I'm perfectly well, thanks. I don't need to be healed!" She was quite unconscious of her handicap!

Many blind friends have been deeply hurt, and have lost faith because they have been subjected to unwise pressure to be healed. "You feel you must be a terrible sinner if, after they have prayed, nothing happens", they say.

We are sure, absolutely sure, that if the Lord wishes, He can heal and restore sight completely, with or without human aid. It just happens, however, that in our experience, He has chosen to use this very blindness to challenge and bless sighted folk in a wonderful way. One of our girls was thrilled when, after years of fretting because she wasn't healed, and after much prayer, she discovered the Scripture in Exodus 4 verse 11; "Who has made man's mouth? Who makes him dumb, or deaf, or seeing or blind? Is it not I, the Lord?"

We met a Christian blind man in his 50s who was praying earnestly to be given his sight. "I believe I shall get my sight back", he said. "Good," we replied. "What will you do when that happens?" "Oh, I'll serve the Lord with all my might, I really will." "What are you doing now?" "Oh, just sitting around, waiting." We urged him to start to serve the Lord now, and not to waste precious time "waiting", but he shook his head, and walked away. He is still waiting.

How much more positive was the attitude of another friend who was also praying and believing he would regain his sight. "I thought," he told us, "when I get my sight, I'll praise and praise and praise the Lord. Then I thought, 'You twit!' Why don't you start praising now!"

We have, oh so much more to learn of the power which God has given us in Christ, so many more wonderful ways to travel, but as we have taken our needs, and the needs of others and spread them before the Lord, we have begun to taste a little of His goodness and grace.

CHAPTER 23 — THE SPOILED STEW

When a group of people live together as a family, then it is inevitable that differences will arise. Even the newborn Church in Acts 2, fresh with the glow of Pentecost, had to face this problem. We have certainly met it. In fact, until we lived together in this way, we had no idea that we ourselves had so many corners which needed to be rubbed off. We became aware of selfishness and impatience which had never been shown in our own home. It made us see how much we needed to be made like Christ. No-one who has not lived in a larger family can really know the self-revelation which such an experience brings. It can be turned to everlasting good if we let the Lord work in our lives.

All that we have written about harmony and fellowship, and times of fun is true. There is tremendous companionship and joy in sharing a home together, yet we need to guard our fellowship, and be vigilant to root out any bitterness which might spoil it.

In II Kings 4:38–41, we read about another family, the family of the Sons of the Prophets. They lived together and ate from the same stew pot. They studied together, built larger premises, and worked happily under the leadership of Elisha. As well as their building projects, they shared the chores. One day they were sent to gather vegetables for a stew. They brought the greens back and put them in the pot. It was not until the stew was served up that they realised someone had been careless, and had gathered a bitter herb by mistake. The

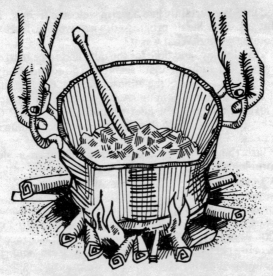

whole stew was spoiled by that one bitter herb—at least that is
what they all thought. But Elisha threw in a handful of meal,
and miraculously, the stew was made wholesome again.

It only takes a little bitterness and criticism to spoil the
warmth of fellowship. But when it appears in the 'stew' it is not
only unpleasant for the one who put it there, it actually
deprives others of the spiritual strength which fellowship
should bring.

"Poor Old Me" is a bitter herb which can be a real nuisance
at times. "My rights" is another tiresome weed which
occasionally appears. "Nobody told ME" is also a likely one in
a family where not everybody is able to be told everything all
the time.

I remember on one occasion we had just returned from a
visit to the regions. We felt rather tired, but were so glad to be
back with our Family. We unpacked, and hurried downstairs
in time for tea.

"Hello, Mum and Dad—lovely to see you back!" Then the
family news had to be told. "Did you know . . . and guess who

called in!'' We certainly had a warm welcome from them all.

But as the meal progressed, we were conscious of something wrong! What was it?

It was Monday, and time for the duty lists to be read out for the week. An audible "ugh" seemed to go round. Duty! No-one *said* it, but it was in the atmosphere that day, and it cast a chill over our home-coming. A poison-weed had crept into our lovely Family. The leader who usually reads out the list felt this attitude so much that she couldn't face reading it, and had to ask a less sensitive person to do it. Poison-weeds are such little things—we seem to rise strong and brave against the big problems of life, yet we are bowled over by the 'little foxes which spoil the vines', the little details which rob us of blessing!

Elisha put a handful of meal in the spoiled stew. Something must be done to sweeten our 'stew' too. We called a special session of prayer, and asked the Lord to help us to see things from His perspective. We received a fresh and joyous recommissioning for His service as we prayed together. The dreaded duty rotas became quite fun, and we didn't have grumbles like that again. The 'Meal' of the wholesomeness of Christ had made the difference.

Those of us in charge felt we had to look closely at what we were expecting from the staff. Were they having opportunities to go out for recreation? Were one or two willing people doing all the extra duties, and wearing themselves out? We and the leaders needed to be very sensitive to these things.

Some of the people on the staff had been used to living in a flat of their own, and of having complete freedom out of work hours. At first, living in a community was very trying for them. They had to help with dishing-out the food at the table, cutting up the meat for a blind colleague who could not manage it alone, pouring out water, fetching favourite sauces, and clearing and laying tables. It was demanding, yet it was also very rewarding, and there was no need to feel lonely and unwanted! However, when work was particularly pressing, it could cause an attack of P.O.M!

We discovered another pressure point too. Tea was over,

and the evening was free for all those personal things which mean so much, such as letter-writing, knitting, sewing, or just relaxing to some favourite music. Then there could come a nagging thought, "Oh dear, I ought to go down to the lounge and have a chat to the visitors." It could spoil any thought of relaxation. There was obviously a need to organise something, so that there was free time for everyone. So we arranged to have hosts and hostesses, who could look after the visitors and the family one evening a week, so that we could all enjoy our free evenings as we liked.

This system works well. The "hosts" bring different ideas into the lounge. Some read a book, or play a game, or have a musical evening. Others just sit and chat. It helps to keep the 'stew' wholesome, too.

Just a few of our blind family seemed to behave very selfishly. Some of the problem was because they couldn't see. They would come to the table, ravenously hungry, eat their first course quickly, and ask for more before the sighted helper had finished dishing out. The fact that the sighted helper was hungry too, and had not had a bite, was not noticed by the blind person. It would be so easy to say impatiently "Don't be so greedy, wait a bit." Just a little patient explanation could result in the blind person developing an awareness of others' needs, which would stand them in good stead wherever they might go.

The business of "my rights" seems to be deep inside us all. "Why should she add a weekend to her week's holiday?" someone remarked impatiently. A bitter herb! Was the speaker being unfairly treated? Did she get her full time off? Or was she just trying to assert her "right" to have all she could get? We never cease to praise God that in this age of insistence on "rights" we have very little problem with this weed. In fact the staff is a constant challenge to me. They have pledged themselves to serve the Lord and to take His yoke upon them, and have gladly forfeited their "rights" for His sake. The "weeds" and "bitter herbs" which spoil the stew are very few. When we think of the many things which could be points of provocation, such as banging doors, night noises, pets and sharing rooms, we are full of praise to the Lord that our life together is so happy.

It is a fact that most of the staff have some difficulties to overcome during their first six months with us. Settling-down in a community can be quite a shattering experience. Many rosy dreams have to be banished in the light of day; preconceived ideas of the romance of serving the Lord have to be adjusted. Also, added to the task of relating to a new family of brothers and sisters, can be the pressure from relatives. "You shouldn't throw yourself away on a job like that! Use your skills to advance yourself." Even the most loving parents find it hard to accept that their son or daughter is devoting training and skill to some obscure mission in this country. They do not understand it as devotion to Christ, unless they love Him too.

There are other bitter herbs which can be gathered all too easily. Praise God, they don't always reach the pot: times when thoughts will take over and say, "Why do you stick around in this crowd? Be a Somebody—you'll never be fulfilled as a person here. Get out!" Usually, it is the individualist who finds this weed a nuisance. It crops up whenever she is tired, or is having to do a part of her job which is routine or boring. What *is* fulfilment? We speak as if it were the pot of gold at the foot of the rainbow. Surely fulfilment for a Christian is to be a "bond-slave" of Jesus Christ—quite the opposite of the world's ideas on the subject.

In spite of irritations and annoyances like—how he drinks his soup—spends his money—how untidy she is in her bedroom —or the big irritation to blind people when someone brushes by them without saying a word— we are able to thoroughly enjoy our "stew" together with very little trouble from "bitter herbs". There is no fulfilment like that of abiding in Christ, and letting Him live out His life in your own. He certainly is the "Meal" which keeps the stew sweet!

CHAPTER 24 — OUTSKIRTS OF HIS WAYS

"Lo these are but the outskirts of His Ways;
and how small a whisper do we hear of Him!" Job 26:14

As we have gone on in the Torch Family we have been humbled to see the blessing experienced by people who we might say are "on the fringe of the Family". The "outskirts of His ways" are encouraging and precious to us. In this chapter we tell of some who have been blessed indirectly through the Torch Family. None of us are in isolation—we all influence others in some way, even if we are but a "small whisper of Him".

Quite apart from the work of bringing the Gospel to blind people and preparing tapes and literature for them, God moves in such gentle ways to bring about His purposes. He promised that those who invited the blind to a feast should be blessed, and we see this happening. Churches which have opened their doors to the handicapped have been richly blessed, sometimes by the witness of blind people, sometimes in ways which cannot be traced to any one person.

We hold our annual Thanksgiving Services in the Autumn of each year, usually in London. But it is difficult to find a suitable church for such an occasion. Either there is no room for coaches to unload blind people, some of them elderly or infirm, or there are not enough toilet facilities, or not enough seating for six to eight hundred people. And the providing of teas is a problem too. As we looked at these difficulties, the minister and deacons of Woodberry Down Baptist Church offered to make their building available to us. They arranged to give us help with the teas, and hired a school opposite for extra teas and toilet accommodation. They cleaned the balcony of their church which was not normally used, and arranged for guides to be available. In fact, they did all in their power to help us. Their help and kindness blessed us, and we were glad to see how much they too were encouraged and rewarded as they looked after us.

Blind people can be a blessing to individuals too. A welfare worker had been visiting an old blind lady regularly. She had often told him about her faith in Christ, and had asked him to read the Bible to her, but he himself did not believe. The old saint was taken to hospital, and it was obvious she was dying. The welfare officer went to visit her. "Please," she asked, "will you pray?" The welfare officer was in a quandary, but he couldn't refuse what might be the old lady's last request. So he prayed. She died peacefully shortly afterwards, but the welfare officer felt that he was a hypocrite. The turmoil inside drove him to make contact with a local Fellowship Group, and later on he found the Saviour for himself.

One day, before we moved, a car drew up in the forecourt at Hurstpierpoint, and a man came to the house. "My wife has read of your work," he said, "and she would like to see what goes on." "By all means" we replied, "bring her in!" "Well, actually she has multiple sclerosis and cannot walk", he said. We brought out our wheelchair, and soon this lady was being shown round by enthusiastic members of staff. "Oh, it's thrilling! I'm so glad I came!" she said.

She began to read children's Bible stories on to cassette for some of the "Spark" readers. Her interest in spiritual things grew. She and her husband met the Saviour, and joined a Church. "My life has purpose now," she said, "even though I am suffering from a terminal illness. My husband too has been blessed. I'm glad I visited you!" She had been touched by the "outskirts of His ways", and had heard His small whisper of peace.

Out in the Fellowship Groups there are many who are touched by the "outskirts", and given a glimpse of Christ. So much love is shown by regional workers, that only in heaven is there a complete record of the blessings given and received there. We only hear of a small part! We have seen the love shown to a young blind woman who had been so protected by her mother that she had not had any education at all. When the mother died, that lady faced a bewildering world. Teaching her to read, to think, and above all, to grow in the Lord, took a lot of patience and time, but it was like bringing someone to life!

A University student volunteered to take a blind man out for the afternoon. He was not a very pleasant man to be with, in fact most people shunned him because he was so dirty. However, he asked to be taken to a Fellowship Group. That student was searching for God, and during the afternoon she found Him.

Sometimes we find ourselves up against helpers who are not helping much at all! One girl was a real trial to us, and we did not know what to do with her. She eventually left to get married. Later she wrote, "I know I couldn't come back to Torch House to work, for I never did a proper day's work. But you taught me so much, and I met love there!" We regarded that episode as a failure, but it was a whisper to a needy heart touched by the "outskirts of His ways."

We gain a great deal from the families which the Lord brings to us, and by individual members of our own families too. When Jill and Paul Ferraby came to live with us, their little boy, Robin, was only 3 months old. The girls were delighted to have a real baby in the house, and followed each development in his life with great interest. When, two years later, brother Alexander came along, they were able to understand the love of parents as they saw the way Paul and Jill patiently helped Robin to become adjusted to life with a baby brother. "Seeing his parents with Robin has helped me no end", said one girl. "I can understand what I missed by not having security and love but, in a way, I'm gaining something from watching Robin."

Family life features quite a lot in the "outskirts of His ways". Several of our staff have seen their relatives born again. One brought her sister to a houseparty, where God

spoke to her. Then the mother, and later the father, came to
Christ. There are still many other relatives of staff who have
no time for the Lord, but we are praying that they too will hear
His whisper.

I have just been counting up, and there are more than ten
couples who are now happily married who met at Torch! Some
met when they came to help for Summer holidays, others
became friends gradually over the years as they worked on the
staff. My father, "Grandad" was the oldest to "meet his
match" this way. He had lived with us for four years, and was a
great blessing to us all. Although he was over 80, yet he would
paint the doors, dig the garden, and help in spiritual ways too.
Then, one day it rained just as he was about to do some
gardening. Dorcas was visiting us at that time, so she took
some mending into the lounge, and they started to chat. When
the rain stopped, we noticed them both walking in the fields.
Sure enough, before that holiday was over, Dorcas and

Granded were engaged! They had two happy years of married life, and I shall never be able to thank the Lord enough, for the way Dorcas cared for my father until he went to be with the Lord. To me, that was a wonderful "whisper" of the outskirts of His ways.

One day, a letter was read in Chapel asking us to pray for a little blind Vietnamese girl who needed a home. Rosina Sharp happened to be in the Chapel that day. It was the beginning of a chain of events which led to the coming of Phung into the family. Something like this has happened again, for a little blind boy has found a home with another of the staff families as a result of a letter coming in to the office. Isn't it exciting to see how God uses even the arrival of a letter at the right time to touch others' lives with blessing?

I can think of people who, unable to go out at all because of ill-health, are a great blessing to us. One old lady prays every day for the Torch Family. She used to crochet and sell little mats and give the money to the Lord's work at Torch. Now her hands will not bend sufficiently to crochet, and her sight is dim, but she still prays for us, and sends a gift regularly from her pension. We can think too of those who work to turn stamps into money for the Lord. One invalid spends hours trimming, sorting and selling stamps. She has made some thrilling contacts in the 'stamp' world, and has been able to witness to some who might not hear of the Lord otherwise. And, each year, several hundred pounds have been brought in to help spread the Gospel to blind people.

We are glad to welcome folk who might be on the "outskirts" into the warmth of the Family, and to share with them the blessings which God is giving. If the "outskirts" are so sweet and precious, what will it be like when we are all together for ever in His presence? It will be glory indeed!

CHAPTER 25 — GEMS FOR HIS CROWN

"Jesus take me as I am,
I can come no other way.
Take me deeper into You,
Make my flesh-life melt away.
Make me like a precious stone
Crystal clear and finely honed,
Life of Jesus, shining through
Giving Glory back to You."

If all the facts could be told about many of the people with whom we have been in contact through the years, what amazing stories would come to light! We want, however, to share just enough for you to see the Hand of God at work, so that we can "give the Glory back" to Him. Because of the intensely personal nature of these experiences, we have re-arranged them so that they do not entirely relate to one person's life, but represent the Lord's working with several who have similar experiences. We see these lives as precious stones which are being shaped in the Master's Hands.

Many people have come and gone in our family circle over the years. We have watched the Master take the most unlikely material, and by long and patient work, bring out hidden depths of beauty which only He knew were there.

Take Sapphire!

Oh what depths of anguish were hidden in Sapphire's body! What passions were buried there. They were constantly tearing at her wherever she went. But no-one would know, for Sapphire had the most amazing self-control. She became introvert and morose, weighted down by all that was heavy within her. She was blind, and craved to be loved, yet seemed to be put in the most loveless of places. Like many others, she had tried on several occasions to end her life. Yet the Master noticed her. He picked her up in His Hands and claimed her as His own. He knew that, hidden in her heart was the deep blue light of love and tenderness, and He wanted to make her into a beautiful gem for His crown. The beauty trapped within her cried out to be released, but the hard rock in which she was embedded was too strong for her to break free. There were rocks of resentment, resentment of men, who had regarded her as a plaything. With a longing for real love such as Sapphire had, this experience had hurt her deeply. So she escaped into a world of fantasy, where everything was happiness, kindness and love. She despised herself for taking refuge in make-believe, and to protect her softer feelings, she did her best to preserve the rocky exterior of resentment, bitterness and pride.

The Good Master began His work. He could see the potential in His chosen stone.

But as tension mounted in Sapphire's rocky prison, one word rang in her mind. "Escape!" But how? Once again, Sapphire looked into the possibility of the final escape of suicide. She carefully planned it all. Pills were easy to come by, and deadly enough when taken in sufficient quantity. Sapphire had quite enough experience in previous attempts to know about them. Sapphire was determined to succeed this time.

Night came, and Sapphire lay in bed. She felt dreadfully ill, but why, oh why had she not lost consciousness? As she lay there, in agony, the Master drew near, near enough to touch her hand. "Oh, My precious child. Why have you done this thing? Why did you try to end the life I gave you? I have deep and wonderful purposes for you—do not faint, but let Me deal with that rocky prison. Only I can release you and bring out that blue fire-gem beneath it. Hold on to Me, My little child, for I understand your need."

Her blind Family surrounded Sapphire with their love, and tried to understand her problems. It was hard to grasp the depths of her mental suffering. Every taunt she had received about her blindness, her habits, her inability to do things quickly, every adverse remark directed at her, seemed to have barbs which entered deep into her soul. All the Family could do was to offer her love.

But the Master knew what to do! Gradually, a ray of light flashed into the dark recesses of her mind, light which was beamed straight from the Master's Face. It found a reflection in her heart. Dear Master! She loved Him, she *knew* she loved Him, and what is more, she knew He loved her. As the beautiful blue of the Sapphire began to flash out, it surprised the whole Family with joy!

From that moment, although the cutting was severe, and many treasured things had to go, the light from the Master's Face was reflected in Sapphire's heart in growing brilliance.

Some day Sapphire will be completely polished, and fit for the Master's crown. Until then, she is growing daily in beauty, and likeness to Christ, and is greatly used in His service.

* * * * * * * *

"There's a path of pure gold
    Filled with promise untold.
    Leading upward to perfect day.
    There's a purpose I see
    That my Lord has for me,
    However perplexing the way."
Surely there was no hope for Emerald!

That she was quick and intelligent no-one would deny, and a stone of precious worth. But who could hope to control that fire? Mental hospital—that was the only answer men could find. So poor little Emerald spent her most formative years in with the mentally sick and the criminally insane. There she tasted communal living at its most crude level. Many treatments were given to Emerald, but none of them succeeded in permanently calming the fire within her. It looked as if she would never become normal.

She longed to be free. She looked out of the window at the cats playing in the hospital grounds—she had just enough vision to see their graceful movements. She would be free like that! So she ran away. But her limited sight and the vigilance of the hospital staff meant that she was soon re-captured and punished. "Show-off" they shouted. "Just an exhibitionist, that's all you are, trying to get attention!" This became the judgment of all who had charge of her. Poor Emerald! What she needed was someone to love her.

One day she heard that God answered prayer, that was all. It was such a slender thread of hope, but she seized it with both hands. "Then I will pray," she said. "God, please get me out of this place!"

Her prayer was miraculously answered. A compassionate teacher of the blind visited her, and arranged for her to be educated away from the hospital altogether. It was what men would describe as a 'gamble'. But the Master-Craftsman had His Hand on Emerald, though as yet she didn't know it.

She was sent to us for the school holidays, and she learned more about the God Who had answered her prayer. She found the Saviour Who had been waiting to claim her.

Then the polishing began.

Most of the rocky mass which surrounded her was made up of fear and emotional wounds. All her life she had been told that she was a nuisance and very selfish. She believed it, for it was easier to do that, and to agree with what people said. At least they didn't argue with her then. But the Master's ways were very different. He saw the true value of His Emerald. He had paid a great price for her—she was not a worthless nuisance. So He surrounded her with a loving family by bringing her to Torch permanently. Love can hurt, however, as it gets under the hardness to the tender part which in Emerald had been hidden for so long. At times her behaviour was most unlovely, as if she must provoke the very ones who were loving her, to test the reality of their love. Because of her bitter experiences, her mind was in a terrible turmoil, crumpled and distraught. Could the Master do anything with Emerald? Could she *ever* be the beautiful precious jewel He wanted her to be? "Nothing is impossible with Me", He said "Just go on loving, love never faileth."

How easy it was to repeat those words, yet the Master had Himself showed us how true they were. Emerald had to be soaked in love, not just for a month, a year, or even two, but for eight long years, before the true worth of this precious gem could be seen. During that period, she ran away many times, and yet was miraculously preserved. Surely her Lord knew the stresses which drove her. She broke windows, smashed cups, and showed many signs of mental disturbance. Yet, through it all shone a deep, growing love for her Lord, and a willingness to do anything He might ask of her. The healing process was gradual, like the polishing of a stone, and Emerald began to sing. Then she set the Family singing as words and music came sparkling from her. The choir became a very precious vehicle for sounding forth the Master's praise, and often the songs came from Emerald.

Physical weakness still dogged her, and it was hard for her to bear, yet through it the Master brought out a tenderness and compassion, and a caring love for others which His fiery jewel might not have had otherwise—for He is producing an Emerald for His crown.

* * * * * * * *

Our Diamond was full of fire! But oh she was so misshapen and in need of the Master's care! A diamond has to be carefully cut and ground down, reduced considerably from its original size so that the polished surfaces can sparkle with light. To do this the mastercraftsman studies the stone closely to find a natural flaw which he can use. Then he sets to work, until he has in his hand a much smaller, but much more beautiful stone than he had before.

It was just like that with our Diamond. She had a very big natural flaw which nearly broke her life. But the Great Master, Who knows His jewels so well, was watching over Diamond.

Her birth was a premature one, and she had to be given oxygen in order to be kept alive. She had too much, and became blind. Her childhood was spent in Children's Homes, mental homes and boarding schools, with an occasional foster home. As she grew up, she became more and more difficult, and even belligerent, though underneath she was very insecure and afraid. The more she stood on the defensive, the more difficult she became, until she was almost uncontrollable. School days were a hopeless failure; she didn't seem able to concentrate. So she turned to the only thing she could do which others found acceptable, and that was to sing. She joined a Group, and travelled around singing in clubs and pubs with the rest. Her 'natural flaw' began to show, for she was a born actress and loved to be praised.

However, singing with the group was hard work. Whatever she felt like, Diamond *had* to sparkle and enthuse the crowds to get the longed-for applause. So she started to take pep pills. Then she went further, until she was injecting drugs before each performance, so that she could be 'high' and carry her audience with her.

The others in the group had also become hooked on drugs. But drugs have to be obtained, and it was while they were trying to get a further supply that the police came. The group ran away, except Diamond, who could not see where to run!

Diamond would prefer to forget the next month or so, except for one event. For it was when she was at her lowest that the Master picked up His jewel. A probation officer, who loved the Lord, came to see her. "Diamond," she said, "Jesus loves you. He died on the cross to take the punishment for your sins. He wants to make you His own child." Love? Diamond was amazed! So someone did love her! Someone understood! She gave her life to Him.

But that was only the beginning. Tenderly the Master held her. What He saw could have dismayed any but the most determined craftsman. For Diamond was in poor shape!

She found that she could use her voice as a Christian. That was fine—everyone wanted her to sing. They liked her testimony too, it was quite sensational. Diamond's natural flaw showed itself again—she became more and more taken up with the praise of men. But the Christian virtues which should have been seen in her as a result of the New Birth were not so evident. Diamond did not seem to understand truthfulness; she used expediency instead. Soon the Christians who had put her on their platforms felt unable to cope with her. Her friends were perplexed. They did not know what was wrong, or how they could help this difficult, unsteady Christian. Diamond longed to pour her heart out to someone. How could she get the better of her lying and selfishness? How could she stop being a sham? How indeed could she come right off drugs?

Then she found herself at Torch house. "Oh dear," she thought, "they are all so 'spiritual' and I am so sensual, so full of lies." But the Master had His Hand on her. He wanted her to be in a loving home so that He could begin His work of shaping, reducing, cutting and dealing with that natural flaw.

Most of her Christian acquaintances did not understand. They never *had* understood Diamond. In their own uncomplicated lives, as soon as a person became a Christian, then all things should change overnight. As this didn't happen to Diamond they tended to ignore her, not because they didn't care, but because they couldn't understand. But her Pastor understood, and that was a great comfort to Diamond. Her friends at Torch House understood too.

So the great Master Lapidary continued His work. There are still many hours of polishing needed to perfect this precious stone, but Diamond is now free from drugs and is learning to draw all the strength she needs from the Lord. She dreads being praised too much in public, and prefers to go out with a team. And how that singing has matured! She doesn't lap-up the applause now, but longs to sing "ever, only for her King".

Under the Master's Hand, we are watching a miracle take place. A rough, faulty lump of stone is becoming a precious jewel, a bright gem for His crown.

* * * * * * * *

There are many other precious lives about whom we could write. The common Agate, rough and unpromising, trodden under the foot of men, is now a thing of beauty, with colours revealed through the polishing which we had no idea were there. And Amber, so easily scratched, so brittle yet so very valuable to the Master—how lovely it is to see her enjoying the Scriptures which once she felt she would never understand.

We are indeed rich with so many precious stones in our family!

CHAPTER 26 — EVERYTHING SHE HAD

The old Guildhall at St. Ives, Cornwall was a hive of activity. Stalls of greengrocery stood, displaying a healthy array of cabbages, carrots, beetroot, and fruit of all sorts. Nearby was a stall selling home-made preserves, pickles, jams

and a mouth-watering array of cakes and sweets. There were stalls with Christmas decorations, balloons, knick-knacks and aprons, beads and brooches, stalls with records and books and, in the centre, an amazing array of hand-knitted garments for people of all ages.

The people of St. Ives poured in as soon as the doors were open, and by early afternoon there was very little left to sell. Near the main door were two stalls depicting the work of the Slavic Gospel Association and the Torch Trust for the Blind, for the whole purpose of this activity was to sell the goods and to give the proceeds to these two missions. For several years now, the money obtained has run into four figures.

When the Missionary Market had closed there was another quick turn-around, as people cleared the Guildhall, and put the seats back in order, ready for the Christian concert to be held that same evening. It was quite a day for some of the organisers!

Each year representatives from the Slavic Gospel Association and Torch go to St. Ives to be present at the Market and the Christian concert, and usually a little team of singers from Torch House takes part in the evening programme.

All very exciting—but how did it start?

The Missionary Market is not like the usual sales of work, and the reason for that lies in the faith and spiritual calibre of its founder, Miss Gladys Major.

We first met Gladys when she was working as a telephonist in London. We had gone to Pembridge Place to speak to a group of Christians who were running a Christian Union there. Gladys was one of the most staunch supporters of that meeting. She had lost her sight when she had a tumour removed, and had subsequently trained and found employment in London. We met Gladys on one or two other occasions when she came down to Crawley to visit us.

Then Gladys started to have a lot of pain in her head, and the Doctor strongly advised her to get out of London to the slower pace of life in St. Ives. That meant, for Gladys, leaving the full and varied life in London, to live in a tiny flat over a greengrocer's shop, with a marvellous view of the harbour which she was not able to enjoy! Gladys was delighted to be back amongst her friends and family, however, and would not have minded the change at all, except that she would have just nothing to do!

But Gladys was a woman of prayer, and she was also very resourceful. If the Lord had ordered her to Cornwall, then she wanted to fulfil all He had for her there!

Gladys had two great loves when it came to Missionary work, one was the Slavic Gospel Association, and its link of love with Eastern Europe; the other was the work of Torch which she had become aware of since she lost her sight. She prayed regularly and in great detail for these two works, and gave too when she was able.

In Carbis Bay, very near to St. Ives, there was a Christian Guest House called 'Lamorna' run by Mr. & Mrs. Richards and Mr. Ian Bull, who were great friends of Gladys. One day the thought was born, "Why not knit dishcloths, oven gloves and cover a few coathangers, and sell them at 'Lamorna', to divide the proceeds between Torch and Slavic Gospel Association." Gladys started straight away. The idea was successful. Holiday makers were glad to buy the hand-knitted goods which Gladys made. Soon she found herself needing some wool. "I prayed about it" she wrote to tell us, "and, do you know, a lady gave me some." The whole venture might have continued like that and never grown to anything more, but local Christians began to be interested, and some of them offered to help. The holiday season was over by this time, so someone suggested doing something for Christmas. Offers came from all directions, as the skills of Cornish men and women were put at Gladys' disposal. Soon a Committee was formed, whose first job was to pray. Gladys did not want just a big sale; she wanted it to be full of the power and blessing of the Lord. And it was! In 1971 the first Missionary Market was held in the foyer of the Guildhall, and was a great success. The Market was opened by Mr. Leslie Edgell of Slavic Gospel Association and Mr. Nick Leonovich, head of Russian Radio Department at Trans World Radio. But all agreed that it was the prayer behind it which made the Market so different from just a money-making effort. The little group of organisers was almost overwhelmed by the success of their venture. They felt as if God had put His seal of approval on their efforts. After much thought and prayer, they decided to hold the Missionary Market the next year, and to follow it by a Gospel Concert in the evening.

The Missionary Market 1972 was again a great success. After the Market was over, the musical talent of the locality came into its own. A choir of 100 lovely Cornish voices, led by Edward Perkin, sang Gospel songs and Cornish carols which delighted the 500 people who crowded in to hear it. This pattern of events has been followed each year, and in 1975 a singing group from Torch joined in the programme, adding their own particular touch to the concert. A few words were spoken by representatives from Torch and Slavic Gospel Association and a word of testimony was given.

That November weekend is anticipated each year with great excitement. Our singers are very keen to be included in the St. Ives party! On the Sunday they visit Churches in the neighbourhood, and receive a warm Cornish welcome, and it is thrilling to meet with the Fellowship Groups which have since grown up in the area.

During the early Summer of 1973, we were near St. Ives on holiday, so we decided to call and see Gladys. She was out when we arrived at her flat, but we were told that she was in a deck-chair on the sea-front. It was a beautiful sunny day and many people were sitting with newspapers over their heads to keep off the sun. We walked the length of the bay, peeping under the newspapers, until we found a braille book doing sunshade duty. Under it was Gladys! She was thrilled to see us, and we had a grand time of fellowship.

Later that summer, Gladys began to suffer from violent headaches. Another tumour had formed, and before the next Missionary Market, Gladys had gone home to be with her Lord.

She left behind her a group of people who had been inspired by her example, and were sure the Lord wanted the work to go on. The Missionary Market is a continuous reminder of a blind lady who, against enormous odds, offered her talents to the Lord.

The poor widow woman in Mark 12 had two mites, but the Lord noticed when she slipped them into the Treasury. He said that she had given something of greater worth than all the rich people who had contributed to Temple funds that day. "She," said Jesus, "out of her poverty has put in everything she had, her whole living." I believe the Lord looked upon Gladys like that, when she offered her whole life to Him in spite of its limitations, and He has blessed her offering to many people.

Truly Gladys has shown us that no life is too restricted to be taken up and used by the Lord in His service. I think we also have a great deal to learn from Gladys when it comes to prayer. She took every need to the Lord, whether it was for onions or knitting wool. I feel she has taught me the value of trusting the Lord for *every* need, however small.

One other direct result of Gladys' efforts has been the forging of strong links between the Slavic Gospel Association and Torch, links which are valued for fellowship, and which have at times been of use in the spread of the Gospel. And all this because one woman was willing to give herself and "everything she had".

CHAPTER 27—CHRISTIAN SERVICE TRAINING

"What is the Lord saying to us?"

We sat in our Leaders' meeting talking over things, trying to understand the way the Lord was leading us. Round us were the men and women whom God had called to be leaders in the work. They had come to mean so much to us, and we valued their prayerful counsel more than we could say. The subject under discussion was that of younger blind people, whose needs seemed to have been brought before us so often of late.

"That is the second phone call we have had this week from Welfare," said Renee, "and both were about young folk who were at a loose end."

"And there was a letter last week, if I remember rightly," added Eileen.

"We've had a lot of letters along the same lines — it's a big need, certainly," said Barbara.

"Well, what are we going to do about it?" exclaimed Nigel, our man of action.

We dropped all the other business and prayed for the Lord to show us His Will.

Many of the new developments in the work of Torch have come about after a particular need has been highlighted, and pressed in upon us through a number of similar requests reaching us around the same time. Then, as we have begun to pray about what we could do, a special case has come before us which has confirmed that the Lord wanted us to develop the work in a new way, or widen our scope to include other areas of need. It was not that one human in distress constituted the call of God, but the constant showing of that same need in many people made us aware of its size. The need for large print came to a head through a deaf-blind lady's plea, though we had heard the plea from many other people before. "Flash" actually came into being through the visit of Lydia from Bethlehem, though we had been thinking about it for a long time before that. "Spark" too had been thought of and prayed about for some time before the little girl phoned us with her plea.

It looked as if something was happening again. The problem area this time concerned young blind people. Some had completed their training and yet were unable to get jobs. Others were in sheltered workshops, doing repetitive work far below their potential. The result was listlessness, discontent, or escape into a world of fantasy. They needed to have incentive, and something creative to do, at least in their leisure hours. The actual case which brought the need to a head was of a girl who had no way of using her little bit of training because she lived in such an out-of-the-way place. She had no company all day except her radio, and no chance to go out, as the rural area in which she lived was almost impossible for a blind person to negotiate. Added to this, she had no hobby to fill the long hours, days, weeks which stretched before her. It was a poor outlook for a girl of 23!

"We must do something for folks like that," we all agreed.

Then the Lord began to work in our minds. He showed us the young folk actually with us at Torch, who had come through many adjustment problems, and who now needed a purpose, an on-going plan to help them to take an active part in life. Why not start with them? Thoughts of a training scheme began to take shape with a definite timetable, including personal management, typing and braille, but majoring on Christian beliefs. We needed to be clear about the purpose of the course. The economic situation in Britain made it almost impossible for them to find a job, and they needed to know how to use their time profitably. We had met many Christian workers who had said to us, "Oh, I wish I could be two people, there is so much to do. If only I had more time." If there was one thing these young people had, it was time! Suppose they could be trained to take their place as Christian workers, voluntary or paid, in the programme of the local church? The thought grew. It was possible. Why, we knew of blind folk who were using their gifts of speaking, reading, music, and even housework in the context of the church. And, if these young people had good basic teaching, they would benefit in their own lives as well.

"That's the answer," said Nigel. "Send them out with the vision to become evangelists."

"Or Sunday School teachers," added Barbara.

"Yes, even caretakers, sick visitors . . .". We were all bubbling over with the vision which was opening up before us.

But it is one thing to have a vision, or dream a dream, and another to see it come to pass. It would require a great deal of prayer and hard work before it could be an established fact. And we only wanted it if it was the will of God! We needed to be certain of that.

We shared our thoughts with the staff. A number of them had qualifications which could prove most useful; in fact it was exciting to find that we had experts to deal with most of the subjects we hoped to cover. The house staff caught the vision too, and began to work out how they could find the necessary bedroom space for new students.

Quite early on, Trevor Welch seemed to stand out as the person most suited to take charge of getting the scheme off the ground. He had experience of management, and had shown a very loving, caring attitude towards students. What is more, he had been in touch with churches over student matters before, and he felt a strong desire to help blind people to play their part in local church life.

Trevor prepared prospectuses and worked out timetables for one academic year, which we thought would be the ideal duration of each course. We were able to put these before two senior officials from the Royal National Institute for the Blind. They knew that there was a big need amongst young people, and were glad something was being done towards meeting it. The fact that our course was essentially a Christian one was an aspect which they understood and accepted. However, it became obvious as we talked, that there would be no chance of any financial help from government departments. Once again, we were undertaking a venture for which we should have to depend entirely on the Lord.

We started to look at the practical side of the project. The staff who were going to be involved in teaching would still have their other jobs to do. Could they cope? Several of the wives had useful skills, but if they were going to give any time to the programme, then something would have to be done about the little children. As things were then, we would need a creche for two hours on three days a week.

There would be the need for paper, braille and large print primers and study courses, and tapes for those who could not read. Desks, work-benches and a room to use for tutorials, all had to be sorted out.

Fortunately, with our production system already at hand, the study courses presented no problem once they had been compiled. Frank dictated the Gospel of Mark onto tape with chapter and verse numbers so that one or two of the students who could not manage braille could begin a Bible Study course. The "Lions" club offered us five reconditioned table-desks, and we curtained off half of what was then the lounge to make a study room for the students.

We felt sure the Lord was in this project the more we prepared for it. In June 1979 we had a trial run of five days with eight of our own young people who were interested in taking the course. They were very keen. Yes, it could work. And so, Christian Service Training, CST, was born.

We planned to start on 1st October 1979 with the eight young people already with us, and three others who were wanting to take the course. All of them were believers. Some had quite a good grasp of the Bible, some had big gaps in their knowledge, and one had only just committed his life to Christ. All of them needed systematic basic teaching, and help in developing their potential in the service of the Lord.

The longing to do something, to be fulfilled, was very strong in those first students. They wanted to learn. Music, crafts, woodwork and cookery were unknown skills to some of them. They talked to us honestly about the things they found difficult. Spelling, writing letters, braille, typing, public speaking and approaching people in an acceptable way, all these were frankly discussed. So often when blind people have approached a youth group or church to try to "belong", they have not been received as they should, because they have been unnaturally extrovert, and the group have felt they must hold them at arm's length. The opposite too has happened. We wanted to train these young folk to take their place naturally in the church. This, to us, would be the path towards fulfilment and true integration.

The churches needed help too to understand the vision we had. Some of the problems connected with integration arose because of ignorance, and fear of upsetting the blind person. "Do you mean we can talk about 'seeing' to blind people?" they asked. Of course, the answer is "Yes; make conversation normally, talk about things as you would to a sighted person". Sighted folk also needed to beware of over-praising a blind person's efforts. "Give praise and encouragement, by all means, but only as it is truly warranted." We have all too often met blind people who have been told they could do things brilliantly, and who have wondered why their skill has not been accepted by everyone. This doesn't help the process of integration with a sighted group, nor, in the end, does it give the visually-handicapped person any confidence in Christian people.

Once launched, the whole scheme brought a new impetus and interest to the staff who were involved. "This CST project is turning out to be a blessing to us all," was the verdict.

But, of course, we did not always sail in calm waters. Individual characteristics soon showed. One girl had the idea that as the early church "had all things in common" so she could help herself to her friends' cosmetics. Then there was the student who complained bitterly about an imagined injustice. We tried to hold up before her the example of our Lord Jesus. "But, Mum Heath, that's just the trouble," she said, "I ain't the Lord Jesus — I'm me."

Over all, that first year was a joy and blessing to everyone. We learned a lot of useful lessons, and found a great deal of hidden talent in our midst. We had fun too!

It was encouraging to see the students' appreciation of the Lord and His grace as they began to mature. Before the course started, several of the students were frightened of any mention of the Second Coming of Christ. At the end of the first term this subject was dealt with in a group study. After the lecture, these very students volunteered, "Oh, how lovely — we're not afraid any more!"

It has been interesting to see the wide variety of young people who have come through the course, all with one aim, to learn more about the Lord.

The CST course is now a well-established part of the scene at Torch House, Hallaton. The staff have rallied wonderfully to this extra demand upon their skills and time, coping with tutorials, lectures, and practical sessions over and above their own work load.

Trevor Welch moved on, leaving the course under the over-all care of Mike Townsend. This entailed liaising with Social Workers, student counselling and guidance. The day-to-day running, programme planning, organising activities and lectures became Hilary's main responsibility. Her work has evolved into a very real caring ministry for students past and present. She has done many quiet acts of love, written letters giving stimulating news, kept in touch by phone, and encouraged those who have gone through the course and are now endeavouring to put into practice what they have learned. The Bible Study notes on Christian Beliefs and Christian Ethics have now been revised and made suitable for use as correspondence courses for young people who are not able to come to Torch House to take the full course. Hilary marks these, and encourages the lone students by her letters.

Has the original vision materialised? Is there any lasting progress in these young peoples' lives as a direct result of the hours spent with them?

Once a year the students come to Torch House for a reunion weekend. Occasions like these give us the opportunity to see how they are getting on, and how they have benefited from the course. We were delighted to see one girl enjoying reading from a braille chorus book. True, she was feeling each dot in a way which showed she had not been a braille reader in her school days, but there she was, taking part in the singing. We remembered when she first came to us. "No, no," she cried. "I can't read braille, they tried to teach me at school and I just couldn't learn. Please don't ask me to learn braille!" We knew that the tiny bit of sight which she had then would soon be gone, and what a pity it would be if she missed the opportunity to learn braille now, while she was young. There were tears, and yet more pleadings. "They told me at school I'd never learn", she cried. We sat her beside one of our blind staff, who patiently took her through the difficult first lessons of reading by "feel". "All right," she said at length, "I'll have a go, but don't be cross with me if I can't do it". We promised we wouldn't be cross, and she began to learn braille in earnest.

Towards the end of the second term, there was a knock on our door. We opened it. There was our reluctant braille reader with two small loaves, one in each hand. "Here you are," she shouted triumphantly, "I read the braille recipe myself, I copied it out for my file, I followed it, and here you are, I've done it!" She had discovered that braille had its uses after all. There are many other practical skills which the students have found of great benefit when they have been able to learn at their own pace. This is specially true of typing, which is so useful to a blind person, as it is a means of communicating with the sighted world.

Students come from a variety of intellectual backgrounds. Some are academically inclined, others can only read with difficulty. But their one intention is to learn all they can about the Lord, and to be better able to serve Him as a result. Such young people are a joy to teach. We shared their excitement as they discovered that the Old Testament was not just a blood-curdling history book, but a wonderful account of God's dealings with man, and a perfect preparation for the stirring events of the New Testament. I'll never forget the gasps of wonder when we read through Messianic Scriptures such as

Psalm 22 and Isaiah 53, so accurately foretelling the sufferings of the cross. "How could I ever have doubted?" said one. Their enthusiasm warmed our own hearts, and caused us to relive the joy of what God had done in giving His only Son to die for us. Students who respond like that are a great joy to teach.

But what of those who are not blessed with academic ability? And how can the two extremes of ability mix? This was a question we asked ourselves at the beginning of one course when we were presented with the widest possible educational gap. It was then that we discovered something!

In the main Christian Beliefs lectures, the students sat together in the same group. There, with the Word of God open before us, those differences of education seemed to disappear. We were a group of people, with one intent, to know more about Him. His Holy Spirit is not a respecter of persons or of abilities. "Blessed are they who hunger and thirst after righteousness, for they shall be filled". Slow learner and fast learner shared the Word, each getting enough to satisfy his needs. When it came to private study times, we gave help to those who found writing answers difficult, but the basic truths of our faith were understood by them all. One poor little lass who came to us was heavily drugged because of brain trouble. All her reactions were slow, and she was not able to learn much in the practical line. She could read very large print with difficulty, and, because of her poor health, we were hesitant about taking her on the course. One of the brighter girls took her under her wing, and helped her with practical things, growing in sympathy and understanding as a result. But, we wondered, was anything going in during the lecture? She always had some answers to offer at the "Talk-back" time, but it was after she had completed the course that we had proof of what it had meant to her. She had been put in touch with the local Torch Fellowship group, who were very kind to her. One day they asked her to tell them about the CST course. She did quite well, describing the subjects taught. Then they said "What would you say is the greatest benefit you have gained from the course?" Her face lit up, and she said, "Oh, I've learned to

208

love Jesus." Most students who come on the course are more able to live normal lives than that little sufferer, but we couldn't wish for a better result.

As we might expect with young people under 30, there is a certain amount of "pairing up". We advise students not to rush into engagements while on the course, as, in the short time they are with us, they need to concentrate to get the best out of the tuition. We remind them of the high rate of divorce, and the appalling breakdown of marriages in our country, and beg them to be careful not to become casualties themselves. Special lectures are given during the course on the subjects of love, courtship and marriage, and advice on matters of sex and family life are covered too. We encourage students to delay any thought of being engaged at least until they have heard these lectures. One couple found this hard. He came from a very poor home, though he was alert and intelligent. He was not a very clear speaker, however, and we couldn't always understand him. She came from a tragically broken home where loving discipline was unknown. They met on the course. From the first, she could understand all he said, and they became firm friends. Towards Christmas, we were told by a conspiratorial whisper in our ear that he had a very special present for her. Gradually it dawned upon us that they were planning to get engaged to each other. As tactfully as we could, because they had not actually told us of their plans, we mentioned the need to wait. Bless them, they did, and at the end of the course, we were able to give them a super engagement party. They were subsequently married, and the social worker responsible for their area phoned to tell us how well they were coping. Two people from sad backgrounds had met the Lord, and were able to establish a Christian home together. These results are an encouragement for us to press on.

However, the path of true love does not always run smooth. Two others who passed through the course, then married, made the mistake of trying to do without any help from welfare sources. Months of muddle and broken hopes wore them down. Even so, they might have pulled through had not the family of one of them intervened. They separated. We were very sad indeed, and we could see how unhappy they were too. We could only pray for them, for it seemed impossible for them ever to get together again. But the Lord worked for them, and they are now happily back together, the wiser for the experience, and linked with a very loving, caring church. We do encourage independence, but it can be taken too far!

We could mention others. Some are now working on our staff, some have been able to find jobs elsewhere. Some have gone on to further studies, and yet others have taken up another scheme which was born as a result of CST. We are referring to the Fleckney Manor Training course, which is run from the Manor House in Fleckney, the home of Mike and Edith Townsend. One or two of the students had many difficulties to overcome, and the course programmed at Torch House was not quite long enough for them to learn necessary living skills. Mike and Edith felt the Lord lay this need upon their hearts, and the result was the very successful training scheme which they have pioneered.

The course at Fleckney Manor is essentially practical, though the spiritual effect of living in a Christian home is considerable. Kay was very afraid of any form of heat when she joined the CST course. Consequently she was not able to reach the level of independence she longed to have. She went to Fleckney, and began to learn how to use a microwave oven. This opened the door for other skills, and eventually Kay was able to live in a flat and completely take care of her day-to-day needs. The flat was at the top of the Manor House, so Edith and Mike were "on call" during those early days of living alone.

Fleckney Manor, however, doesn't provide permanent housing, but prepares students to live on their own. Finding homes in the right environment for these young people is fraught with difficulties, and we wonder what the Lord wants us to do for them. Some form of sheltered housing would seem to be the answer. Is this the next area the Lord is asking us to enter?

Fleckney is only eleven miles from Hallaton, so we are still able to have contact with the students, and it is good to see them developing so well. Some of the blind staff at Torch

House have been able to go over to Fleckney for instruction in household management, in preparation for marriage, or for living alone. So the bond which unites the two houses is a very close one. In a real sense we can serve one another.

We live in a very insecure world. It is tragic to hear of the way blind people have been taken advantage of. The "kind" gardener who turns round and robs, the false friend who makes free with the money, these are stories which come to us all too frequently. We endeavour to help our students in both courses to cope with living in this sick world, and, most of all, to contribute to the Christian witness in their own areas.

As one of the successful students was leaving for home, he said, "You know, my Christian Service Training isn't ending today — it will go on all through my life."

If all the students continue to learn and serve the Lord all their lives, then the CST course will indeed have been worth while!

Fleckney Manor

CHAPTER 28—VISION AHEAD

It was nearly midnight, and the Committee had been in session since 6.30 pm.

"There are so many things we have to decide in a hurry," complained one of the members, "and others which we have had to leave because they need to be prayed through."

"Why don't we arrange a special weekend to do all these things? We might even find time to enjoy each others' company, too."

All the members of the Committee felt that this was a suggestion which was prompted by the Lord. So a date was arranged there and then.

There were many matters to discuss. The leaders of each department of the work had written out their thoughts and ideas, and their own vision for the future. It was heartening, and very revealing. All of them needed more room and better equipment; some were short of staff, and others felt that they would have to do more drastic re-organising to meet the need of visually-handicapped people more adequately. They all looked to us for direction.

We had been pressed to sell some of our land to developers, and the prospect looked inviting. A little capital would be a bonus considering the needs we were facing, especially as the land in question was a rather weedy vegetable plot. Yet, somehow, we held back. Should we sell land which the Lord had so obviously given to us? But maybe He gave it to us to sell! We had discussed this matter for some months, and had come to no real conclusion. We needed time to consider it and above all, to pray the matter through together.

The weekend started with a Committee Meeting on the Friday evening. Several matters requiring decisions were deferred until a longer time could be spent considering them. So it was on the Saturday that we began to tackle these problems and sought God's will for the work in its broadest sense.

We began to read from Romans chapter 11 verse 33, and read through to the end of chapter 12. The reading directed our thoughts to the greatness of God, and challenged us to present our bodies to Him for loving, self-giving service as we played our part in the Body of Christ.

After prayer, a number of matters were talked through and agreed upon — it seemed easier to see the right pathway when we were free from the pressure of time. We considered computerization, and realised it was necessary for the future developments needed. It would obviously help with finance and envelope addressing, but would also be invaluable for braille production programmes, especially where foreign braille was involved, cutting out the tedious correcting of zinc plates, and speeding up the production of the Scriptures in many foreign languages. What a thrill it would be to be able to supply our overseas friends with the Scriptures they so much wanted. The thought of computerization was exciting.

But computers have a "language" of their own, and they need to be programmed. Who could steer us through the many problems involved in computerizing braille, especially foreign languages? God had wonderfully prepared for this very need, for our colleague, Mike Townsend, had a doctorate in Computer Science. Mike not only understood the "language", but was able to guide us through the many technicalities involved, such as which computer would "speak" to our equipment in the right way. Also Edith, his wife, is fully qualified in this field. So they began the process of finding out what equipment would be best, and how to do the necessary programming for foreign languages. Our friends in the Christophel Blindenmission were very interested in this venture, even to the point of helping to buy some of the equipment needed. The problem of programming a computer to convert a foreign language such as Russian into braille was mastered by our friend Professor Don Rogers. He and Mike worked on this, and with the help of others who had a good knowledge of the language the problem was overcome.

So the computerization began. At first the path ahead was fraught with difficulties, as the old Marburg braille plater objected to being driven by a computer. In fact it literally "went to pieces". However, when these difficulties were eventually overcome, the door swung open for us to print braille Scriptures in many different languages. With fast-printer facilities, our whole braille programme has become very versatile. We remembered that years ago the Lord had said to us: "Give ye them to eat". Now, as never before, we were equipped to do just that.

During our weekend of prayer, we looked at other departments too. We began to see that there were areas of outreach which we had not explored for the giant size print which we produced. Now that we were using photo-typesetting, hymn books, Scriptures and other Christian literature could be produced more effectively. Public libraries were interested, as there are visually handicapped people in every town, and some of them are looking for Christian literature in this very large print. It is our vision ahead to be able to meet this need.

We took a long look at each department in this way at that memorable weekend, until all points had been covered except the proposed "development of the vegetable plot". Agents wanted to develop land owned by the Vocation Sisters, and they could make a more lucrative proposal for planning permission if they could have the use of our land too.

We discussed the situation at great length, and prayed yet again. It became clear eventually that we were not to consider making money on that land, but to use it to provide much-needed staff accommodation instead.

It is hard to describe the utter peace which came into all our hearts after we had decided this. Once again, we had been offered a tempting substitute to what God had to give us. How essential it is that we wait and trust Him to show us His plan. It is always so much better than ours!

And the time did come for us to develop that vegetable plot. We were able, using a "kit" system, to erect two cosy bungalows, thus enabling us, Mum and Dad Heath, and Frank and Jean Meech, to move out of the main house, leaving the flats there for newly-weds and other staff bedrooms. And we still had planning permission for two other dwellings as well. In fact, within the year, work was going ahead to put up the house which the Ferraby family now occupy.

Meanwhile, the production department was fast running out of room, and the prospect of computerization meant that the premises would have to be extended. Those unsightly ruins by the main gate were the obvious place for any expansion of the production complex.

However, there were other priorities to consider. An Act of Parliament early in 1985 set a standard for students, and those having any sort of care, which was impossible for us to comply with as we were. It was stated that those in care should have bedrooms 108 square feet in area, with fitted washbasins. None of the bedrooms we were using were the required size, though they were all very well fitted. That was one problem. Added to it was another. At Regional Conferences, and some of our houseparties, we overflowed the dining room and had to have two sittings for meals. This posed problems when organising the programmes, and was very difficult to arrange from the cooking point of view. We were growing out of our home! Looking forward, we realised that as the production work grew, so there would be need for more helpers and staff, some of whom would need to live in the house. The tape department and the libraries were overflowing too. What was to be done? We needed to pray, and then, after that, to plan. As we waited on the Lord, the answer gradually began to formulate. A new wing would be needed combining an extension to the library, and including a dining room, and a larger kitchen, with bedrooms above. The plans reached the drawing board stage when an architect friend, a fellow believer, offered his services free of charge. So the project has begun to take shape.

The plans include twenty bedrooms which will meet the requirements of the law, and a lift for those of our visitors who are not able to manage stairs, extended library areas, and a new kitchen and dining room. The extended library areas will make possible another vision which has for some time been in our minds. As more visually-handicapped people are becoming involved in Christian Service, resource materials are needed for special areas of study. Ministers and others wishing to prepare Bible Studies could be given the opportunity to use the libraries for the necessary resources. With tape recorders at the ready, brailling machines, and even a "reader" on call, we could open up to others the facilities available at Torch House itself.

But such a building project is bound to pose a few problems. Finance, for one! Yet, as we have begun to pray, indeed, from the moment we decided to draw up plans, the Lord has begun to touch our finances. We have had extra gifts which have enabled us to renovate windows and roof areas which were becoming troublesome. We even began to build up a small Development Fund. The Lord has never led us to have a large bank balance, it is very much "His Hand to our mouth" financially, except when He is planning some major development. We experienced this when we were preparing for the move up to Hallaton, now it seemed to be happening again. The huge amount needed for the completion of our plans is not a problem if we are moving in the centre of the will of God.

Another problem was voiced by some friends: "We'll be too big to keep the family spirit". This has always been a personal anxiety to me, because the family is such an essential part of the ministry of Torch. But "family spirit" doesn't depend so much on numbers as on attitudes. When we are bound together by the deep bond of love in our Lord Jesus Christ, then we shall not lose that oneness and that caring which is the characteristic of family life. There have to be guidelines in every big family, but we try to avoid making unnecessary rules. Instead we prefer to try to "By love, serve one another". God has brought several couples to work with us who are only too willing to use their homes to foster this family attitude. It is thrilling to see the way they so willingly share in loving and caring for people who might otherwise be a little "out of it".

Other practical problems will have to be faced as well, for the office, tumbledown as it is, stands on the site required for the new development. Where could we move the administration side of the work? As the office complex was a temporary building constructed forty years ago, the problem of re-housing it would have to be faced in any case sooner or later.

Perhaps the biggest problem in our minds as we look ahead is that of having enough finance to finish the job. Supposing we should start and then not have enough money to finish! This is where we have to look back at the mercies of the Lord in His dealings with us in the past. He has proved to us again and again that He is a God Who works miracles. In fact He is always ready to show His power, if we will trust Him, and walk in the centre of His will.

One of the most recent memories which strengthened our faith at this time was the way the Lord provided for the Ferraby home. Jill and Paul Ferraby and their three children had for some years been living in a one-bedroom flat in Torch House. As the children were growing up, this situation became more and more difficult. In the end, Paul was sleeping on a bed in his studio. This was not good, so we prayed to the Lord, and He provided enough money for us to put a deposit on a "kit" similar to that used for the bungalows, to enable us to build a house. When the "kit" came we were required to pay the balance of the cost, £20,000, by the end of the next month. There was nothing in the kitty! Three weeks went by, and we kept praying for the Lord to show us what to do. I'm afraid some of us felt the chill of doubt creeping into our hearts. But Dad seemed absolutely sure that the Lord wouldn't let us down. Then the phone rang. "You don't know me, but I've just sold my late sister's house for Torch, and it has realised £23,000 — you'll be having a letter from the solicitor any day now." What a relief! What joy! We were sorry we ever doubted our Lord. Now a lovely house stands in the grounds as a monument to the goodness of the Lord. No, He Who is our Guide, will not leave us unable to complete the project.

What should we do with the old dining room and kitchen? That would not be a difficult problem to solve! Ever since we moved from Hurstpierpoint to Hallaton we had longed for somewhere comparable to the little purpose-built chapel which meant so much to us when we were there. How we missed the atmosphere of quietness, when we could draw aside from the bustle of our working life to the peace of a place which was dedicated to that one purpose. The room we use as a place of worship now is also used for other things, and at times it is far from quiet! We could envisage the old dining room with its panelled walls as fulfilling this need, with the servery adapted to serve as a vestry, a small room in which counselling could be done. As for the kitchen, that could be a very useful coffee lounge, thus relieving the present congestion in the coffee bar.

As we tried to look at this project from all angles, we began to realise that it would cause quite a lot of upheaval. But what was the alternative? We were already having to say "no" to a number of people who wanted to come, because we had not enough suitable accommodation, and how could we say "no" to the call to provide Christian literature to nations where blind folk were waiting for God's Word in their own tongue? We realised we had no choice.

Planning an extension which will pass all the rigorous demands of councils and fire regulations is no easy task, yet if the outcome is that many more people will be able to be strengthened in Christ, and brought to know Him, then it will all be well worth while.

So much of this has evolved since that weekend of prayer, but we look back to that time with gratitude, for truly the Lord will lead us if we will let Him.

* * * * * * * *

It has never worked, in Torch experience, to sit down and plan in minute detail where the work might develop. Take Fellowship Groups as one example. A friend once opened a map of Britain before us, and, pointing to the principal cities, he said, "You want to start up here, then there. Plan round the most strategic areas, and your work will grow." But it didn't work like that — it never has done in Torch. We can have ideas, but the final plan is usually something we have not imagined at the planning stage. It is just as well, for if Dad and I had known in 1959 what the Lord had in store, we should have been terrified!

Truly, Fellowship Groups and their little sisters, Prayer Groups do not conform to a pattern. Beyond certain obvious guidelines, each Group is able to function as the Lord leads the people who are committed to that Group. So some Groups have a very clear evangelistic ministry, whereas in others, the accent may be on Christian fellowship, and spiritual strengthening of believers. Prayer Groups were originally designed to pray towards starting a local Fellowship Group. However, some have found it impossible to hold a monthly meeting, and so have concentrated on visitation, caring, and literature distribution, just as a fully-fledged Fellowship would do. Yet, on our records, it still remains a Prayer Group. Most Prayer Groups do develop into Fellowship groups, of course, but as needs vary from area to area, so the development of a Group can vary too. One thing we endeavour to ensure is that all those involved in policy making should be truly born again, and faithful to the principles laid down in the Scriptures. We have often advised that even the drivers should be committed Christians, but the Lord has surprised us more than once.

Many of the local groups are hard pressed to find Christian drivers who can find time once a month on a Saturday afternoon to transport people to the Fellowship Group, so they have been glad to enlist the help of other kind people who are not committed Christians. One such driver took an elderly blind couple twenty-two miles to a Torch Fellowship Group every month for a year or more. One day he was pouring his heart out to his passengers, telling them all his troubles. One of them leaned forward and said, "You know, you need Jesus. He can help you". That was all. It rang in his ears again and again, until he found his way to the Saviour. That man is now leading a Torch Fellowship Group in the area where he lives, so the couple no longer have to travel each month to attend a Group.

The links which Torch Fellowship Groups have with Torch House are often strengthened when folk from a Group receive a call from God to come and work at Hallaton or Hurstpierpoint. Many young people have given us valuable time between courses, and have gone back home with a real vision for the work locally. Others come from the Fellowship Groups to stay!

Bill was one of those kind people willing to help out occasionally by taking blind people to the Group. His wife was a Christian, but Bill was not. He decided to help the local Group to show that "you don't have to be a Christian to do good". One very wet day, he took some folk to the Group. One of the passengers was a dear old lady who could only walk with difficulty. "Oh," she said as she leaned on her frame, "You don't know what it means to me to come here each month". Bill couldn't forget that remark. What was it that was so precious to this woman? As he sat in that meeting, the Lord met with him. Bill became a Christian. And it was all or nothing with Bill. After much prayer and thought, he and Irene joined us at Torch House for a week. Bill was given the job of partitioning a small room. "Help!" Bill thought, "this is way beyond my skills." But he prayed as he worked, and the result was just right. Some months later, Bill and Irene and their son Allan came to work with us on a permanent basis. We said a heart-felt "thank you" to that Fellowship Group. And, as you can imagine, the links between us have grown even stronger. There are new Groups constantly forming in the UK. Sometimes people meet to pray for a while before we hear of them. At other times such Groups are born as a direct result of deputation activities or visits of the choir. We have long since stopped trying to plan where a Group should be formed, but rather have prayed for the Lord to move the hearts of His children everywhere to be made aware of the needs of visually handicapped people around them.

There is still a very big unmet need among the 150,000 visually handicapped people in Britain, but when we think of future plans, we know we have to "roll up" the map and let the Lord do the leading.

One of the ministries which God is using more and more is that of music. We have been blessed with a number of talented people who can sing, or compose, or play an instrument. Consequently teams frequently go out to take part in Church worship, or visit clubs for the blind, or disabled folk seeking to spread the message of the gospel. Some, such as Sandy, have an obvious evangelistic ministry. As people listen to the testimony of the teams, whether in word or song, we have seen the hand of the Lord reaching out to the most unlikely people. Prisoners, youngsters in schools, as well as Fellowship Groups, have been blessed by the ministry of music. Sometimes the choir will go out on a ten-day outreach, when a whole area can be visited and the work be made known in an area where there is no Fellowship Group or where the existing Group needs more support. We find too that such efforts bring new needs to our notice. There are potential readers everywhere. One young man was struggling to keep his own business going, though his wife had left him. He said, "I'm not a Christian like you people, but I like to be with you. I wish I could study the Bible. Have you anything in braille which would help me?" We had. On another occasion I held the tiny hand of a blind baby. What would those little fingers be reading in later years? The faith and joy of his Christian mother and father was a great blessing to us. Again, we were glad that we had a literature programme which included the very young.

Compact cassettes are being used increasingly these days. As well as the obvious ministry of music and song, programmes containing short talks, poetry and dramatic presentations of the Scriptures are able to reach many people who, for one reason or another, have limited concentration. This door is wide open, the only limits are those of time, equipment and personnel.

There is so much more ground to be covered. The deaf-blind in Britain are a small minority, but their needs make them a priority. We should love to do more for them.

In these days, children who are visually handicapped are not always educated in special schools but may be integrated into the sighted education system. This, though good in some ways makes it harder for us to contact them.

Young folk, and working blind people need a different approach to encourage and interest them. They are often attracted to organised holidays like those at Keswick and the Holy Land. Adventure holidays too appeal to the teenagers who are fit and active.

* * * * * * * *

Future vision would not be complete without mentioning the overseas outreach. Friends from abroad have joined us for several houseparties at Torch House, and we have linked with them for similar gatherings in Norway and Spain. The result of such fellowship is a widening of our horizons, and a precious sharing of Christ with those of other nations. Mind you, this often results in extra work finding its way to the production department. "Could you print Psalms in Swedish braille for us please?" Or it might be that a hymn book is wanted, or a young people's chorus sheet.

As we mentioned earlier in this book, we held a conference at Hallaton in 1976 at which there were preliminary discussions concerning braille production of the Scriptures world-wide. This was followed up by a conference held at Darmstadt in 1983, when world need was further analysed, and areas of responsibility defined. We were "allocated" West Africa and Eastern Europe, and since then have acquired India as well. Mike and Edith and Don Rogers attended that conference, and were able to assist in formulating the most convenient lay-out for braille Scriptures, to ensure that they were easy to read from a blind person's point of view. There is a real cry for such Scriptures and the computerised programmes make it much more possible for us to help. This too is all part of "future vision".

We do not know how long we have before our Lord returns, but He has told us to "work for the night is coming when no man can work". So we want to be alert to His leading as we reach out more and more to visually handicapped people world-wide.

What about future leadership of the Torch family? Many times we, as Mum and Dad of the family have been asked if we are retiring. As we have repeatedly taken this matter to the Lord, we have felt strongly that He will show far more definitely than is evident at present if and when He wants us to retire. We thank Him daily for health, and we thank Him too for the splendid team of leaders who are taking their share of responsibility in their own departments in a very dedicated way. The whole work can function whether we are physically here or not. Committee members take an active part in certain aspects of the work too. Mike Townsend has taken over the needs of students and staff when dealing with official matters. He is also deeply involved in the computer side of things, and has the over all running of Fleckney Manor Training too. But Mike, like ourselves, cannot do everything. He would be the first to say how much help and support he gets from the leaders. Some of the younger folk who have been through deep personal battles are now keen to help in ministering to others. They have the Torch Family spirit very much at heart.

It would be impossible to give detailed plans of the way ahead. Maybe the Lord will never provide another Mum and Dad for the Torch Family, but give instead a group of dedicated brothers and sisters to carry out the vision in the future. Meanwhile we pray for clear thinking, divine widsom, and the courage to follow the Lord wherever He may lead.

Hallaton House showing the proposed extension

POEM FOR OPEN DAY 1980

Only a little acorn
Yet it grew into a tree.
Fed and watered by rain and snow,
Wind and sun, all made it grow.
Cold frosts of adversity
These made the tree.

Torch had a small beginning too
Almost hidden from men's sight
But, nurtured by the Lord each hour
By His great Spirit's wondrous power
The flame burned bright
Though dark the night,
And lives were changed when Christ came in
To free the heart from self and sin.

That first lone book in braille became
A well-stocked library.
Then magazines began to be
Published to keep them company.
And still more booklets now are planned
To put into each eager hand
Throughout the world.
India, Africa, Russia, from lands afar, the cry
Comes, "We want braille Christian booklets—all you can supply."

As for the Large Print and the Tapes,
They'll increase too, we know.
Electronic gremlins MAY do their worst;
Yes, we *do* need more staff who will put God first.
Yet, in spite of every blow, the Gospel Light WILL go
To the old, and the lonely, in hospital ward.
Through Large Print and Tapes, they will hear God's Word.

Only a small beginning
In Birmingham, ten years ago,
Yet, by the Power of God alone
Torch Family Fellowship Groups have grown.
And, like a torch, held high, light flows
To old and young, and life bestows.
From Aberdeen to Cornwall, from Glasgow down to Kent,
The saving Power of Jesus is very evident.

And now we have the C.S.T.
That's growing like a tree,
Training that is giving
A purpose clear for living.
Maybe the group is small
But students have heard God's call,
They want to give Him all
And serve Him well.

If only one blind person
Will see the Saviour too,
And be transformed from darkest night
Into the joys of heavenly light!
This is the deep desire of all
Who work with Torch at the Master's call.
REJOICE, work on, for it is plain
Your work of love is NOT IN VAIN.

(S. G. HEATH)

If you wish to receive *regular information* about *new books*, please send your name and address to:

London Bible Warehouse
PO Box 123
Basingstoke
Hants RG23 7NL

Name..

Address ....

....

....

....

I am especially interested in:
☐ Biographies
☐ Fiction
☐ Christian living
☐ Issue related books
☐ Academic books
☐ Bible study aids
☐ Children's books
☐ Music
☐ Other subjects

P.S. If you have ideas for new Christian Books or other products, please write to us too!

Other Marshall Pickering Paperbacks

THROUGH DAVID'S PSALMS

Derek Prince

Derek Prince, internationally known Bible teacher and scholar, draws on his understanding of the Hebrew language and culture, and a comprehensive knowledge of Scripture, to present 101 meditations from the Psalms. Each of these practical and enriching meditations is based on a specific passage and concludes with a faith response. They can be used either for personal meditation or for family devotions. They are intended for all those who want their lives enriched or who seek comfort and encouragement from the Scriptures.

LOVING GOD

Charles Colson

Loving God is the very purpose of the believer's life, the vocation for which he is made. However loving God is not easy and most people have given little real thought to what the greatest commandment really means.

Many books have been written on the individual subjects of repentence, Bible study, prayer, outreach, evangelism, holiness and other elements of the Christian life. In **Loving God**, Charles Colson draws all these elements together to look at the entire process of growing up as a Christian. Combining vivid illustrations with straightforward exposition he shows how to live out the Christian faith in our daily lives. **Loving God** provides a real challenge to deeper commitment and points the way towards greater maturity.